31 BATTLE CRY DECLARATIONS

DESTINY IMAGE BOOKS BY TROY A. BREWER

Redeeming Your Timeline: Supernatural Skillsets for Healing Past Wounds, Calming Future Anxieties, and Discovering Rest in the Now

Looking Up (Updated & Expanded Edition): Understanding Prophetic Signs in the Constellations and How the Heavens Declare the Glory of God

40 Breakthrough Declarations: Powerful Prayers to Heal Past Hurts, Make Future Provision, and Invite Jesus into Your Timeline

31 BATTLE CRY DECLARATIONS

POWERFUL PRAYERS AND DECREES THAT RELEASE SUPERNATURAL BREAKTHROUGH

TROY A. BREWER

DESTINY IMAGE® PUBLISHERS, INC.
P.O. Box 310, Shippensburg, PA 17257-0310
"Publishing cutting-edge prophetic resources to supernaturally empower the body of Christ"

This book and all other Destiny Image and Destiny Image Fiction books are available at Christian bookstores and distributors worldwide.

For more information on foreign distributors, call 717-532-3040.

Reach us on the Internet: www.destinyimage.com.

ISBN 13 TP: 978-0-7684-7785-6

ISBN 13 eBook: 978-0-7684-7786-3

For Worldwide Distribution, Printed in the U.S.A.

1 2 3 4 5 6 7 8 / 28 27 26 25 24

CONTENTS

Introduction

Remember the Alamo!

My fascination with Texas history in general, and the Alamo in specific, began my seventh-grade year. An eighth-generation Texan, I was born to do battle. I was especially born to be a freedom fighter. My birthday is December 6, 1966, a day that seems to be stamped by winning the battle for freedom.

December 6, 1956, is the day Nelson Mandela was arrested for opposing apartheid in South Africa. He eventually became the Prime Minister of that nation and abolished that demonic practice. It's also the day Harriet Tubman escaped from slavery in 1849, and the exact day in 1865 when the 13th Amendment that abolished slavery in the United States was passed.

December 6, 1963, is the day President Lyndon B. Johnson, also a Texan, bestowed the Presidential Medal of Freedom on 31 recipients, including his predecessor John F. Kennedy, who died fighting the good fight against the globalist elite.

So what is the "good fight"? The one you wage to overcome evil and bring freedom to the oppressed. That's why I love to remember the Alamo. You don't have to be black to revere Dr. Martin Luther King Jr., or Catholic to love Mother Teresa. Just like that, you don't have to be a Texan to love the men who fought and died trying to defeat the evil Mexican dictator Antonio Lopez de Santa Anna.

I've read dozens of books on the battle and visited the site more than 50 times. Every time, my tripped-out mind sees Davy Crocket still atop those adobe walls, firing against all odds. William Barrett Travis is fighting for his life and legacy on the cannon platform at the northeast corner of the fortress despite looming defeat.

Standing on that hallowed ground, the Lord God gave me a download. He said, "Troy, make sure you're on the right battlefield, because if you're fighting on the wrong battlefield, you have no grace to win."

The revelation struck me like a lightning bolt. Sure I had heard people say, "Pick your battles carefully," and "Is this the hill you want to die on," but understanding the Lord actually has battles lined up for me that He has destined me to win, was a game-changer. It was a sobering moment to learn that not every battle was mine and I would get my hat handed to me if I stepped onto someone else's battlefield. Right then and there, I knew the Alamo was the wrong battlefield for those 189 brave Texan defenders.

What was the right battlefield? It happened 46 days later. How I love the victory of the Battle of San Jacinto. I often visit that battlefield and imagine Sam Houston on his white horse in full gallop toward Santa Anna's tent. He was so far in front of the other Texas freedom fighters that his horse got shot out from under him and he kept right on advancing yelling, "Remember the Alamo!"

Defeat is costly. Remembering that cost is what fueled Houston and won the day. Oh, the fight for freedom! There is something special about those who battle darkness so they can unlock the chains of others in bondage. I have noticed that while not all revolutionaries are godly people, godly people are always revolutionaries. We love freedom!

Yes, a true characterizing of the love of God is to hate bondage and oppression because we love what He loves and hate what He hates (Proverbs 8:13). Psalm 111:10 says that the fear of the Lord is the beginning of wisdom. It takes the fear of the Lord and plenty of wisdom to know which battlefields belong to you.

REMEMBER THE CROSS

Nearly 2,000 years before the freedom-fighting Texans fell at the Alamo, Jesus Christ was lifted on the cross. He hated oppression and bondage to sin (the devil) so much that He was willing to die to overcome it.

He loved humanity and wanted you and I to be set free so badly, He was willing to give up His own life to give us a shot at true freedom. Get this straight: Jesus is not your warden. He is your Deliverer. The Bible says that whom He sets free is "free indeed"!

> It is for freedom that Christ has set us free.
> Stand firm, then, and do not let yourselves
> be burdened again by a yoke of slavery.
> —Galatians 5:1 NIV

It is my humble opinion that Jesus is the only way to have the freedom to forgive, to have joy and peace, to love, and to pursue a life of passion that makes a difference to your own life and the lives of others.

Because you are reading this book, you are battling for freedom. You are fighting the good fight and you're looking for tools and encouragement to win the day. You have found them in these pages. These prayers, Scriptures, and declarations are what I use daily to wage war against every kind of hell coming against me. I can tell you that the Isaiah 11:2 Spirit of the Lord is all over these words because they are His words.

My friend, you are more than a conqueror. You are an overcomer. Know that this book will help you go behind enemy lines to take out the weapons fashioned against you. You'll drag prisoners of war out of that camp and earn the victor's crown. The gates of hell will not prevail against you. You are the devil's worst nightmare because you will stand at those hellish gates and redirect traffic!

Though Jesus has already won the war for your freedom, it's up to you to win the daily battles the enemy wages in your heart, mind, family, finances; the list is long, but know that you are on the right battlefield when you invite Jehovah Nissi—the Lord our Banner—to ride onto your battlefield and display the King's flag over your life. He loves to fight for you and to give you the credit for the victory.

The war for freedom has been won! Our ongoing battles with the bully of darkness is to remind us of this victory and our need to uphold God's glory. When that molester of souls comes around, remind him that he's not only defeated—you have the keys and authority to lock him up.

Troy

1

BATTLE CRY FOR PROPHETIC DREAMS AND ENCOUNTERS

He said, "Listen to my words: 'When there is a prophet among you, I, the Lord, reveal myself to them in visions, I speak to them in dreams'" (Numbers 12:6 NIV).

Father God, You have invited me into a place of intimate encounter with your heart. You are my King and my Bridegroom—the one who utters secrets into my soul and lifts me into higher places with You. Your Word says in Proverbs 25:2 that it is the glory of God to conceal a matter, but it is the honor of kings to search out that matter.

Jesus, give me the honor of a king to search out the wonderful mysteries You have for me to find. Show me great and mighty things I do not know (Jeremiah 33:3). Give me ears to hear Your voice day and night. Lord, I give You permission to speak into my dreams and proclaim the identity, purpose, and destiny You have created just for me. I am not afraid of my future but run toward it and toward You.

Jesus, I surrender myself to Your Holy Spirit that I might bring Heaven to earth and comfort, strengthen, and encourage those who need You most. Here I am— send me! I invite Your Kingdom to come and Your will to be done in my heart through dreams, visions, words of knowledge, and prophetic encounters. I pray all this in Jesus's mighty name. Amen.

SCRIPTURES

Psalm 19:1-2 (NKJV) – *The heavens declare the glory of God; and the firmament shows His handiwork. Day unto day utters speech, and night unto night reveals knowledge.*

Joel 2:28-30 and Acts 2:17 (NKJV) – *And it shall come to pass afterward that I will pour out My Spirit on all flesh; your sons and your daughters shall prophesy, your old men shall dream dreams, your young men shall see visions. And also on My menservants and on My maidservants. I will pour out My Spirit in those days. And I will show wonders in the heavens and in the earth: Blood and fire and pillars of smoke....*

Job 33:14-18 (NKJV) – *For God may speak in one way, or in another, yet man does not perceive it. In a dream, in a vision of the night, when deep sleep falls upon men, while slumbering on their beds, then He opens the ears of men, and seals their instruction. In order to turn man from his deed, and conceal pride from man, He keeps back his soul from the Pit, and his life from perishing by the sword.*

Revelation 1:12-13 (NKJV) – *Then I turned to see the voice that spoke with me. And having turned I saw seven golden lampstands, and in the midst of the seven lampstands One like the Son of Man, clothed with a garment* *down to the feet and girded about the chest with a golden band.*

Psalm 126:1 (NKJV) – *When the Lord brought back the captivity of Zion, we were like those who dream.*

Daniel 2:26-28 (NKJV) – *The king answered and said to Daniel, whose name was Belteshazzar, "Are you able to make known to me the dream which I have seen, and its interpretation?" Daniel answered in the presence of the king, and said, "The secret which the king has demanded, the wise men, the astrologers, the magicians, and the soothsayers cannot declare to the king. But there is a God in heaven who reveals secrets, and He has made known to King Nebuchadnezzar what will be in the latter days. Your dream, and the visions of your head upon your bed, were these."*

Daniel 1:17 (NKJV) – *As for these four young men, God gave them knowledge and skill in all literature and wisdom; and Daniel had understanding in all visions and dreams.*

Genesis 20:3 (NKJV) – *But God came to Abimelech in a dream by night, and said to him, "Indeed you are a dead man because of the woman whom you have taken, for she is a man's wife."*

Psalm 3:5 (NKJV) – *I lay down and slept; I awoke, for the Lord sustained me.*

Psalm 4:8 (NKJV) – *I will both lie down in peace, and sleep; for You alone, O Lord, make me dwell in safety.*

Genesis 40:8 (NKJV) – *And they said to him, "We each have had a dream, and there is no interpreter of it." So*

Joseph said to them, "Do not interpretations belong to God? Tell them to me, please."

Matthew 2:19 (NKJV) – *Now when Herod was dead, behold, an angel of the Lord appeared in a dream to Joseph in Egypt.*

Daniel 7:1 (NKJV) – *In the first year of Belshazzar king of Babylon, Daniel had a dream and visions of his head while on his bed. Then he wrote down the dream, telling the main facts.*

Genesis 41:25 (NKJV) – *Then Joseph said to Pharaoh, "The dreams of Pharaoh are one; God has shown Pharaoh what He is about to do."*

I DECLARE IN THE MIGHTY NAME OF KING JESUS:

- When I seek God, I find Him. When I ask, He answers; and when I knock, the door is open unto me.

- I am a prophetic dreamer with the gift to understand and interpret dreams.

- My mind at night belongs to God and I will see and hear Him speak in my dreams.

- When I'm awake, I welcome visions, prophetic words, and supernatural encounters.

- I will make myself available to God through my dreams. When He speaks, I will say, "Here I am."

- I will remember my dreams. I will steward my dreams correctly. I will write them down and tell testimonies of the Most High God.

- I live a supernatural lifestyle of dreams and encounters—this is normal for me.

- I bring the miraculous wherever I go because the Holy Spirit resides in me.

- I am a prophetic speaker bringing words of strengthening, encouragement, and comfort to all.

- Jesus has opened doors for me no one can shut. He has given me keys to Kingdom advancement, wisdom, and knowledge.

- The words of my mouth and the meditations of my heart are in line with His Word and heart.

- The Lord has assigned angels to carry out the prophetic words I am given.

- I am in alignment with the Kingdom. I will not miss the visitation of the Lord.

2

BATTLE CRY FOR VICTORY OVER CURSES, VOWS, AND INIQUITIES

Out of the same mouth proceed blessing and cursing. My brethren, these things ought not to be so (James 3:10 NKJV).

Father God, I know You love me and have blessed me. You have never cursed me but see me as complete through the blood of Jesus. Knowing that, I reject all curses that have come against me from the lips of others and from my own words spoken in self-defeat. I refuse to believe the lies brought against me, and I forgive those who have spoken against me and my future.

Lord, I ask You to examine my bloodline. See if there is any iniquity passed down to me. Break off any leftover curse so I may be counted among the thousand generations of those who love You. I also ask You to search me for any inner vows I have made—vows that I "will never," "can't," "refuse to," or "I won't." I know that when I say such things, I am making a commitment to something other than You. This takes the future out of Your hands for me and my children. Forgive me, Lord! I repent of my careless words that not only stall my purpose and destiny, but cut off my generations from all that You have for them.

Jesus, I ask forgiveness for the grumblings and curses I have spoken in anger or carelessness over the lives of my family, friends, and even my enemies. I repent! I will not partner with hell through my words. Holy Spirit, move in me! Give me a clean heart to forgive those who have wronged me so that bitterness and evil words will not come from my lips. I pray for a heart that speaks blessing over my enemies and honor over those I love. Let me prophesy in love for the strengthening, encouragement, and comfort of myself and others. I ask this in the mighty name of Jesus. Amen.

SCRIPTURES

Lamentations 5:7 (NKJV) – *Our fathers sinned and are no more, but we bear their iniquities.*

Deuteronomy 30:19 (NKJV) – *I call heaven and earth as witnesses today against you, that I have set before you life and death, blessing and cursing; therefore choose life, that both you and your descendants may live.*

Leviticus 26:40-42 (NKJV) – *But if they confess their iniquity and the iniquity of their fathers...if their uncircumcised hearts are humbled, and they accept their guilt—then I will remember My covenant with Jacob, and My covenant with Isaac and My covenant with Abraham I will remember....*

Numbers 14:18 (NKJV) – *The Lord is longsuffering and abundant in mercy, forgiving iniquity and transgression; but He by no means clears the guilty, visiting the iniquity of the fathers on the children to the third and fourth generation.*

Romans 3:12-14 (NKJV) – *...There is none who does good, no, not one. Their throat is an open tomb; with their tongues they have practiced deceit; the poison of asps is under their lips; whose mouth is full of cursing and bitterness.*

Jeremiah 32:18 (NKJV) – *You show lovingkindness to thousands, and repay the iniquity of the fathers into the bosom of their children after them—the Great, the Mighty God, whose name is the Lord of hosts.*

2 Corinthians 10:5 (NKJV) – *Casting down arguments and every high thing that exalts itself against the knowledge of God, bringing every thought into captivity to the obedience of Christ.*

Proverbs 18:21 (NKJV) – *Death and life are in the power of the tongue, and those who love it will eat its fruit.*

Ephesians 4:29 (NKJV) – *Let no corrupt word proceed out of your mouth, but what is good for necessary edification, that it may impart grace to the hearers.*

Luke 6:45 (NKJV) – *A good man out of the good treasure of his heart brings forth good; and an evil man out of the evil treasure of his heart brings forth evil. For out of the abundance of the heart his mouth speaks.*

Matthew 5:34-35,37 (NKJV) – *But I say to you, do not swear at all: neither by heaven, for it is God's throne; nor by the earth.... But let your "Yes" be "Yes," and your "No," "No." For whatever is more than these is from the evil one.*

Matthew 7:1-2 (NKJV) – *Judge not, that you be not judged. For with what judgment you judge, you will be* *judged; and with the measure you use, it will be measured back to you.*

James 5:9 (NKJV) – *Do not grumble against one another, brethren, lest you be condemned. Behold, the Judge is standing at the door!*

I DECLARE IN THE MIGHTY NAME OF KING JESUS:

⸸ I am of the bloodline of Jesus. All curses spoken against me are null and void because His blood paid for my complete and full redemption.

⸸ The future of my children is blessed by my words and attitudes, that no iniquity would be passed down through my generations. I am a chain breaker!

⸸ All inner vows I have made that limit my purpose and destiny and the future of my children are broken. They are cancelled by the blood of Jesus.

⸸ Any judgments I have made against others are cast down. Jesus is the only Righteous Judge.

⸸ I forgive those who have hurt me and refuse to walk in any form of bitterness, whether by grumbling, inner vows, or curses. I break any partnership with the sons of Korah or the House of Dathan.

⸸ I am not a clanging gong! I speak with love and prophesy for the empowerment, healing, and comfort of others.

✝ I will bless those who speak against me and pray for their hearts to be turned to the truth. I will not return curse for curse.

✝ I am a life-breather. I refuse to speak negative words that lead to death.

✝ Every evil imagination is cast down. I will bring every thought into captivity before they become words or actions.

✝ I repent of judgments, grumbling, careless words, curses, and vows. I will seek and speak forgiveness because I want to live by the fruit of the Holy Spirit.

✝ I declare love and self-control over my thoughts, words, and actions. Where I once saw death from my words, I will now see life manifest throughout my relationships and works.

3

BATTLE CRY FOR SUPERNATURAL SANITY

And do not be conformed to this world, but be transformed by the renewing of your mind, that you may prove what is that good and acceptable and perfect will of God (Romans 12:2 NKJV).

Father God, I ask You to invade my soul. Show me any wayward thought or evil imagination in me. You know my thoughts (Psalm 139:2) and I ask You to convict and correct me so I may be trained in Your righteousness (2 Timothy 3:16). Because the heart is desperately wicked, search me, Lord, and root out any wicked way in me (Jeremiah 17:9). Jesus, train me to set my mind on things above and not on the things of the earth (Colossians 3:2).

I commit my works to You so you can establish my thoughts (Proverbs 16:3). Because I am made in Your image, You have given me the mind of Christ. Lord, cause my mind to meditate on Your goodness and those things that are excellent so I can bring Heaven to earth for those around me. Compel me to put on the helmet of salvation to protect me from the lies of the enemy and to take up the sword of the Spirit, which is Your Word to guide me (Ephesians 6:17). With these weapons, I stand against the wiles of the enemy—who was defeated at the cross. I will withstand the evil day and be called victorious (Ephesians 6:13). I take every thought captive and hold it up to You, King Jesus, that I would not be conformed to this world, but be transformed by the renewing of my mind today and every day (Romans 12:2). Amen.

SCRIPTURES

Philippians 4:8 (NKJV) – *Finally, brethren, whatever things are true, whatever things are noble, whatever things are just, whatever things are pure, whatever things are lovely, whatever things are of good report, if there is any virtue and if there is anything praiseworthy—meditate on these things.*

2 Corinthians 10:5 (NKJV) – *Casting down arguments and every high thing that exalts itself against the knowledge of God, bringing every thought into captivity to the obedience of Christ.*

1 Peter 1:13 (NKJV) – *Therefore gird up the loins of your mind, be sober, and rest your hope fully upon the grace that is to be brought to you at the revelation of Jesus Christ.*

1 Corinthians 2:12 (NKJV) – *Now we have received, not the spirit of the world, but the Spirit who is from God, that we might know the things that have been freely given to us by God.*

Luke 6:45 (NKJV) – *A good man out of the good treasure of his heart brings forth good; and an evil man out* of the evil treasure of his heart brings forth evil. For out of the abundance of the heart his mouth speaks.

2 Timothy 1:7 (NKJV) – For God has not given us a spirit of fear, but of power and of love and of a sound mind.

Ephesians 4:22-23 (NKJV) – That you put off, concerning your former conduct, the old man which grows corrupt according to the deceitful lusts, and be renewed in the spirit of your mind.

Philippians 4:6-7 (NKJV) – Be anxious for nothing, but in everything by prayer and supplication, with thanksgiving, let your requests be made known to God; and the peace of God, which surpasses all understanding, will guard your hearts and minds through Christ Jesus.

Romans 10:17 (NKJV) – So then, faith comes by hearing and hearing by the word of God.

James 3:14-17 (NKJV) – But if you have bitter envy and self-seeking in your hearts, do not boast and lie against the truth. This wisdom does not descend from above, but is earthly, sensual, demonic. For where envy and self-seeking exist, confusion and every evil thing are there. But the wisdom that is from above is first pure, then peaceable, gentle, willing to yield, full of mercy and good fruits, without partiality and without hypocrisy.

Proverbs 17:22 (NKJV) – A merry heart does good, like medicine, but a broken spirit dries the bones.

Proverbs 15:28 (NKJV) – The heart of the righteous studies how to answer, but the mouth of the wicked pours forth evil.

I DECLARE IN THE MIGHTY NAME OF KING JESUS:

✟ I am quick to hear, slow to speak, and slow to anger.

✟ The fruit of the Spirit is evident in my words and actions. I demonstrate love, joy, peace, patience, kindness, goodness, faithfulness, gentleness, and self-control in all I do and say.

✟ My words bring real life and transformation to the lost and hurting. They bring freedom to the captives of sin and death.

✟ You have made me mighty for the pulling down of strongholds and the casting down of evil imaginations and lofty opinions that go against the knowledge of You, Lord.

✟ I will not be deceived. I do not talk to snakes nor will I partner with the "in-a-me" in my thought life.

✟ I do not think or speak curses over myself or others. I do not make inner vows that lead to iniquities for my family, my generations, or those around me.

✟ I have a repentant heart. I seek and give forgiveness with a ready apology when my words miss the mark.

✟ I bring every thought into captivity in obedience to Christ.

✟ The words of my mouth and the meditations of my heart are acceptable to You, Lord.

✟ I rejoice with those who rejoice and weep with those who weep. My hope is in You.

✝ My inner self is being renewed day by day because You have given me the mind of Christ.

✝ I turn away wrath with a soft answer and refuse to stir up anger with harsh words.

✝ I am a disciple of Christ Jesus and I know the truth. Because I know the truth, Jesus has set me free.

4

BATTLE CRY FOR VICTORY OVER UNFORGIVENESS AND BITTERNESS

Bearing with one another and, if one has a complaint against another, forgiving each other; as the Lord has forgiven you, so you also must forgive (Colossians 3:13 ESV).

Heavenly Father, I know You have forgiven me so much. I come before You asking for forgiveness for my inability to forgive others. Fill me with Your love and compassion for others. Give me Your heart and Your eyes to see them as You do (1 Samuel 16:7). Your Word says all have sinned and fall short of Your glory (Romans 3:23). I have no room to judge because we all have faults and require forgiveness. I repent of my inability to forgive and ask You to tear out any bitter root in me that causes trouble and defiles those around me (Hebrews 12:15).

Jesus, I know that holding a grudge is like drinking poison every day hoping it will make the other person sick. It does nothing but kill my own faith, hope, and testimony. I will not take the name of Christ in vain through bitterness, and proclaim I will be reconciled to those who have hurt or offended me before I come to the altar with my prayers and praise (Matthew 5:23-24).

I know You cannot forgive me or hear my prayers if I refuse to forgive those who have trespassed against me (Matthew 6:14-15), so Holy Spirit, cause me to be slow to anger and quick to forgive that this would result in righteousness (James 1:19-20). Cause me to refrain from bringing up old conflicts through selfish pride. Lord, break that pride off and give me a spirit of humility, love, and a sound mind. I know that You, who are Love, keep no record of wrongs (1 Corinthians 13:4-7) therefore, I refuse to dwell on the wrongs I have suffered but give them to You. I will forgive 70 x 7 times because You have commanded it (Matthew 18:21-22) for my good. Thank You, Lord Jesus. I pray this in Your name. Amen.

SCRIPTURES

Psalm 103:12 (NKJV) – *As far as the east is from the west, so far has He removed our transgressions from us.*

Matthew 6:12,14 (NKJV) – *And forgive us our debts, as we forgive our debtors. ...For if you forgive men their trespasses, your heavenly Father will also forgive you.*

Matthew 18:21-22 (NKJV) – *Then Peter came to Him and said, "Lord, how often shall my brother sin against me, and I forgive him? Up to seven times?" Jesus said to him, "I do not say to you, up to seven times, but up to seventy times seven."*

Matthew 18:27, 32-33 (NKJV) – *Then the master of that servant was moved with compassion, released him, and forgave him the debt. ...Then his master, after he had called him, said to him, "You wicked servant! I forgave you all that debt because you begged me. Should you* *not also have had compassion on your fellow servant, just as I had pity on you?"*

Mark 11:25 (NKJV) – *And whenever you stand praying, if you have anything against anyone, forgive him, that your Father in heaven may also forgive you your trespasses.*

Luke 6:37 (NKJV) – *Judge not, and you shall not be judged. Condemn not, and you shall not be condemned. Forgive, and you will be forgiven.*

Acts 2:38 (NKJV) – *Then Peter said to them, "Repent, and let every one of you be baptized in the name of Jesus Christ for the remission of sins; and you shall receive the gift of the Holy Spirit."*

Ephesians 4:31-32 (NKJV) – *Let all bitterness, wrath, anger, clamor, and evil speaking be put away from you, with all malice. And be kind to one another, tenderhearted, forgiving one another, even as God in Christ forgave you.*

Colossians 3:13 (NKJV) – *Bearing with one another, and forgiving one another, if anyone has a complaint against another; even as Christ forgave you, so you also must do.*

1 John 1:9 (NKJV) – *If we confess our sins, He is faithful and just to forgive us our sins and to cleanse us from all unrighteousness.*

I DECLARE IN THE MIGHTY
NAME OF KING JESUS:

✝ I bring all offenses to the foot of the cross. Jesus, You are the righteous judge and Your Word says You will repay any wrong done to me.

✝ I run to forgive others because I have been forgiven. God's mercy and grace flow freely to and through me.

✝ I no longer count people's wrongs against them and refuse to hold a grudge. No bitter root will grow up in me!

✝ Christ empowers me to give others what I have received from Him. That includes forgiveness.

✝ Jesus is my strength in every struggle. The devil no longer overpowers me.

✝ God's love and forgiveness are my strongest attributes. I am a warrior for forgiveness.

✝ I refuse to drink the poison of unforgiveness which only punishes me. Because of this, the Lord hears my prayers.

✝ I am free from the anger, guilt, and bitterness of unforgiveness. I refuse to revisit past offenses against me.

✝ I am not a curse to others. I seek forgiveness from those I hurt or offend with speed and humility.

✝ I run to the throne of grace when I fall or fail. I do not hide my sin from You, Lord. I admit it and readily repent.

Because You have forgiven me much, I will forgive others and walk in the freedom of a clean heart.

5

BATTLE CRY FOR VICTORY OVER DEPRESSION

When the righteous cry for help, the Lord hears and delivers them out of all their troubles. The Lord is near to the brokenhearted and saves the crushed in spirit (Psalm 34:17-18 ESV).

Holy Spirit, I break the claim the enemy has over my heart and mind. Deliver me from this dark place and these dark thoughts. By Your stripes I am healed in my heart, mind, and emotions (1 Peter 2:24). You are a shield about me—my glory and the One who lifts my head from the pain and isolation of depression (Psalm 3:3).

Because of Your love, my soul is not downcast. I have put my hope in You and will praise You, my Savior and my God (Psalm 42:11). I am not hopeless because my hope is not in people or possessions. My hope is in You, Jesus (Psalm 39:7). When I feel alone, I have confidence in Your presence. You promise to never leave nor forsake me (Deuteronomy 31:6). I am Your servant, friend, child, and the bride of Christ. I have all of Your love and all of Your attention. I do not have to share You because You are limitless. I will not mistake exclusiveness for loneliness.

Lord, I know You go before me and are with me. You will never leave me nor forsake me. Because of this, I will not be afraid or discouraged (Deuteronomy 31:8). Because You see me as righteous, I cry out to You, Holy Spirit, and You will deliver me from my troubled thoughts and emotions (Psalm 34:17). When I wait patiently for You, You turn to me. You hear my cry and lift me out of the mire. You set my feet on the rock—a firm place to stand. I thank You for the new song You have put in my mouth (Psalm 40:1-3). The joy of the Lord is my strength (Nehemiah 8:10) and the fruit of the Holy Spirit are mine! Thank You for delivering me, Jesus. Amen.

SCRIPTURES

Psalm 23:4 (NKJV) – *Yea, though I walk through the valley of the shadow of death, I will fear no evil; For You are with me; Your rod and Your staff, they comfort me.*

Psalm 9:9 (NKJV) – *The Lord also will be a refuge for the oppressed. A refuge in times of trouble.*

Proverbs 3:5-6 (NKJV) – *Trust in the Lord with all your heart, and lean not on your own understanding; in all your ways acknowledge Him, and He shall direct your paths.*

Proverbs 12:25 (NKJV) – *Anxiety in the heart of man causes depression, but a good word makes it glad.*

Isaiah 41:10 (NKJV) – *Fear not, for I am with you; be not dismayed, for I am your God. I will strengthen you. Yes, I will help you. I will uphold you with My righteous right hand.*

Jeremiah 29:11 (NKJV) – *For I know the thoughts that I think toward you, says the Lord, thoughts of peace and not of evil, to give you a future and a hope.*

Matthew 11:29 (NKJV) – *Take My yoke upon you and learn from Me, for I am gentle and lowly in heart, and you will find rest for your souls.*

2 Corinthians 1:3-4 (NKJV) – *Blessed be the God and Father of our Lord Jesus Christ, the Father of mercies and God of all comfort, who comforts us in all our tribulation, that we may be able to comfort those who are in any trouble, with the comfort with which we ourselves are comforted by God.*

Philippians 4:8-9 (NKJV) – *Finally, brethren, whatever things are true, whatever things are noble, whatever things are just, whatever things are pure, whatever things are lovely, whatever things are of good report, if there is any virtue and if there is anything praiseworthy—meditate on these things. The things which you learned and received and heard and saw in me, these do, and the God of peace will be with you.*

2 Timothy 1:7 (NKJV) – *For God has not given us a spirit of fear, but of power and of love and of a sound mind.*

I DECLARE IN THE MIGHTY NAME OF KING JESUS:

- My feelings are liars. The Word says the heart is desperately wicked, so I will not let my emotions rule me. Knowing the truth of Jesus has set me free.

- I have the mind of Christ. The enemy has no place in my thoughts. I am set free, delivered, and healed.

- I am not ruled by fear or discouragement. I live daily with renewed hope in my God-anointed future.

- Nothing is too big for my Lord and I to handle together.

- I am a warrior against the ways of darkness and evil. I do not talk to snakes or entertain vain imaginations of any kind.

- I see and perceive the goodness of God in the land of the living. The Holy Spirit has brought me real life and transformation.

- I live with an everlasting hope that fills me with joy. The Lord is my stronghold and place of rest.

- I take every thought captive and turn it over to the loving authority of Jesus.

- I am an empowered overcomer. The joy of the Lord is my strength and my victory song. The devil is a liar and I crush him under my heel.

- Because You are the Prince of Peace, chaos and confusion are defeated. They have no place in my thinking.

✝ I have the mind of Christ and have been made mighty for the pulling down of strongholds and casting down of evil imaginations that rob me of my God-given joy.

6

BATTLE CRY FOR VICTORY OVER ANXIETY, FEAR, AND WORRY

Do not be anxious about anything, but in every situation, by prayer and petition, with thanksgiving, present your requests to God. And the peace of God, which transcends all understanding, will guard your hearts and your minds in Christ Jesus (Philippians 4:6-7 NIV).

Father, I know that humans are born into trouble, as sure as sparks fly upward (Job 5:7). The world is full of trouble and anxiety. Jesus says in John 16:33 (NIV), "I have told you these things so that in me you may have peace. In this world you will have trouble. But take heart! I have overcome the world." Lord, help me to cast all my anxiety on You because You care for me. Only Your shoulders are big enough to carry my concerns. Give me the confidence to know that through You, I can receive victory in every part of my life. Thank You, Lord, "that greater is he [the Holy Spirit] who is in me, than he [the enemy] that is in the world" (1 John 4:4 King James Version).

Jesus, give me the assurance that You will never leave me nor forsake me (Hebrews 13:5). Cause me to not borrow trouble from tomorrow and worry about the future. Give me Your strength to follow Matthew 6:34, where Jesus says not to worry or be anxious about tomorrow, for tomorrow will have worries of its own. I will seek You and Your Kingdom because You will work out every part of my life, giving me Your peace, comfort, and love.

Lord, commission Your angels to surround me with Your protection and direction. Take over in the anxious parts of my life and, by faith, I will trust that You will dispel the enemy for my good and Your glory. Be my Prince of Peace. Have dominion in my heart and mind. I ask all these things in the mighty name of Jesus. Amen.

SCRIPTURES

Psalm 94:19 (NKJV) – *In the multitude of my anxieties within me, Your comforts delight my soul.*

Proverbs 12:25 (NKJV) – *Anxiety in the heart of man causes depression, but a good word makes it glad.*

Isaiah 26:3-4 (NKJV) – *You will keep him in perfect peace, whose mind is stayed on You, because he trusts in You. Trust in the Lord forever. For in Yahweh, the Lord, is everlasting strength.*

Matthew 6:25-27 (NKJV) – *Therefore I say to you, do not worry about your life, what you will eat or what you will drink; nor about your body, what you will put on. Is not life more than food and the body more than clothing? Look at the birds of the air, for they neither sow nor reap nor gather into barns; yet your heavenly Father feeds them. Are you not of more value than they? Which of you by worrying can add one cubit to his stature?*

Matthew 6:34 (NKJV) – *Therefore do not worry about tomorrow, for tomorrow will worry about its own things. Sufficient for the day is its own trouble.*

John 16:33 (NKJV) – *These things I have spoken to you, that in Me you may have peace. In the world you will have tribulation; but be of good cheer, I have overcome the world.*

Philippians 4:8-9 (NKJV) – *Finally, brethren, whatever things are true, whatever things are noble, whatever things are just, whatever things are pure, whatever things are lovely, whatever things are of good report, if there is any virtue and if there is anything praiseworthy—meditate on these things. The things which you learned and received and heard and saw in me, these do, and the God of peace will be with you.*

Colossians 3:15 (NKJV) – *And let the peace of God rule in your hearts, to which also you were called in one body; and be thankful.*

2 Timothy 1:7 (NKJV) – *For God has not given us a spirit of fear, but of power and of love and of a sound mind.*

James 3:18 (NKJV) – *Now the fruit of righteousness is sown in peace by those who make peace.*

1 Peter 5:7 (NKJV) – *Casting all your care upon Him, for He cares for you.*

I DECLARE IN THE MIGHTY
NAME OF KING JESUS:

- I will not allow myself to worry or be full of anxiety because the Prince of Peace rules over my heart and mind.

- I have faith to cast all my cares on Jesus because He cares for me.

- No weapon fashioned against me shall prosper because I am an overcomer. Victory is mine.

- I rest in the promises of God's Word to never leave me nor forsake me.

- I pray about every concern and am determined to know I am in God's capable, loving hands.

- I trust in the consolation of God's logos and rhema words.

- I thank You, Jesus, for the answers to my concerns before I see them with my eyes.

- I walk by faith, believing God to bring me good things.

- I refuse to listen to the lies of the enemy. Devil, you are not the author or the finisher of my faith. I will not be defeated by a defeated devil.

- I refuse to be afraid of my future because the Lord holds my future in His hands. He is good.

- I am called to be a child of the light. There is no darkness in me.

✝ I am not a worrier. I bring hope to the lost and hurting through Jesus Christ, my Savior.

✝ The Holy Spirit rising up in me enables me to operate in boldness, love, and a sound mind.

✝ Because I have seen God work for good in my life, I can trust Him with my future. I will not fear because His ways are good.

7

BATTLE CRY FOR VICTORY OVER ANGER

*...Everyone should be quick to listen, slow to speak and slow
to become angry, because human anger does not produce the
righteousness that God desires* (James 1:19-20 NIV).

Lord, I know that outbursts of anger are not a good witness for You and Your Kingdom. Forgive me for the times I acted as a fool without patience or self-control. Jesus, You are the Prince of Peace. Rule and reign over my thoughts and words. Have dominion over my actions. Holy Spirit, I desire the fruit You offer—love, joy, peace, patience, kindness, goodness, faithfulness, gentleness, and self-control. I give You permission to calm the storm that rages in me. Just as the wind and waves obeyed Your command, so will my soul obey Your Word over my life. Because You've forgiven me for all the times I trespassed against You, I forgive those who have wronged me. Father, tear out any bitter root that is keeping me from truly loving and selflessly serving others.

Transform my thinking and the words I speak. Make them words of life, strength, and encouragement. Holy Spirit, I give You permission to convict and correct me when I respond in anger and not in love. Lord, make me an overcomer in all areas of my life. Fill me with Your love and with self-control. Make me like You: compassionate and gracious, slow to anger and abounding in love. Jesus, cause me to respond in love, to speak with a soft answer, to offer kindness, and to see others as You do, Lord. Teach me to overcome evil with good that my end shall be peace. In Jesus's name I pray. Amen.

SCRIPTURES

Proverbs 16:32 (NKJV) – *He who is slow to anger is better than the mighty, and he who rules his spirit* **[is stronger]** *than he who captures a city.*

Psalm 37:8-9 (NIV) – *Refrain from anger and turn from wrath; do not fret—it leads only to evil. For those who are evil will be destroyed, but those who hope in the Lord will inherit the land.*

Proverbs 15:1 (NKJV) – *A soft answer turns away wrath, but a harsh word stirs up anger.*

Proverbs 22:24 (NIV) – *Do not make friends with a hot-tempered person, do not associate with one easily angered.*

Proverbs 29:11 (NLT) – *Fools vent their anger, but the wise quietly hold it back.*

Ecclesiastes 7:9 (NLT) – *Control your temper, for anger labels you a fool.*

Matthew 5:22 (NLT) – *But I say, if you are even angry with someone, you are subject to judgment! If you call someone an idiot, you are in danger of being brought* *before the court. And if you curse someone, you are in danger of the fires of hell.*

Luke 6:31 (NLT) – *Do to others as you would like them to do to you.*

Romans 12:19, 21 (ESV) – *Beloved, never avenge yourselves, but leave it to the wrath of God, for it is written, "Vengeance is mine, I will repay, says the Lord." ...Do not be overcome by evil, but overcome evil with good.*

Ephesians 4:26 (ESV) – *Be angry and do not sin; do not let the sun go down on your anger.*

Colossians 3:8 (NIV) – *But now you must also rid yourselves of all such things as these: anger, rage, malice, slander, and filthy language from your lips.*

I DECLARE IN THE MIGHTY NAME OF KING JESUS:

† The Prince of Peace rules over me. He has dominion in my thoughts, words, and actions so I will glorify the name of Jesus.

† I have the fruit of the Spirit—love, joy, peace, patience, kindness, goodness, faithfulness, gentleness, and self-control—in every part of my life.

† I have the mind of Christ. I speak words of affirmation, praise, and encouragement to myself and others.

† I do not talk to snakes but crush them under my heel.

✝ I will show forth justice, mercy, and walk humbly before my God.

✝ I refuse to hold a grudge when someone speaks or acts negatively to me. Jesus forgave me all my sins. Likewise, I forgive those who wrong me.

✝ I am an ambassador of Heaven, and I have a higher calling. Anger has no hold on me.

✝ I will repent and bring any anger outburst to the foot of the cross before sundown. Anger is for fools, and I am wise in Christ.

✝ I yield my body, mind, and soul to the Holy Spirit. He is my Comforter, Counselor, and ever-present Help in times of trouble.

✝ I am free from the sin and shame of my past. I am quick to apologize and ask forgiveness of all I may hurt or offend.

✝ Jesus has given me the wisdom and means to cancel every debt against me.

✝ Vengeance belongs to the Lord. I will not steal what is His through anger or selfish retribution. He has defeated my enemy and the "in-a-me" of anger.

8

BATTLE CRY FOR VICTORY OVER ADDICTION

Yet in all these things we are more than conquerors
through Him who loved us (Romans 8:37 NKJV).

Father, I thank You that You are lifting me up. You have not let the foe of addiction rejoice over me. You are bringing my soul up from the grave that I will not go down into the pit of despair (Psalm 30:1-2). Deliver me from my destructive behavior (Psalm 107:20). Jesus, I know You are the only cure for the sins that have so easily entangled me (Hebrews 12:1). I am calling on You— seeking You with all my heart. Rescue me. Break off the chains of addiction and help me to stand on the solid rock of Jesus. I renounce the sinking sand of temptation (Matthew 7:24-27) and declare the fruit of the Spirit in the places I have been defeated (Galatians 5:22-23). I have no other gods before You (Exodus 20:3).

Lord, today I return to You—my Stronghold. I am a prisoner of hope who claims Your promise that I will be restored doubly to You (Zechariah 9:12). I am weary and heavy-laden of the guilt and shame of my addiction. I pray today for Your rest (Matthew 11:28-30). Deliver me from my affliction, Holy Spirit. Let my faith in You make me well (Mark 5:34). Father, I claim a right mind filled with love and self-control. I gladly put on the full armor of God so I can stand against the schemes of the enemy (Ephesians 6:11). Because I know You will never tempt me and will always give me a way out of temptation, I will look for and take every escape route You put before me (1 Corinthians 10:13). I will not give the enemy opportunity or permission to devour me (1 Peter 5:8). You have made me to be an overcomer, and I look forward to sitting beside You on Your throne (Revelation 3:21).

SCRIPTURES

Proverbs 23:20-21 (NKJV) – *Do not mix with winebibbers, or with gluttonous eaters of meat; for the drunkard and the glutton will come to poverty, and drowsiness will clothe a man with rags.*

Proverbs 25:28 (NKJV) – *Whoever has no rule over his own spirit is like a city broken down, without walls.*

Isaiah 5:22 (NKJV) – *Woe to men mighty at drinking wine. Woe to men valiant for mixing intoxicating drink.*

Hosea 4:11 (NKJV) – *Harlotry, wine, and new wine enslave the heart.*

Luke 21:34 (NKJV) – *But take heed to yourselves, lest your hearts be weighed down with carousing, drunkenness, and cares of this life, and that Day come on you unexpectedly.*

Romans 8:37 (NKJV) – *Yet in all these things we are more than conquerors through Him who loved us.*

1 Corinthians 6:9-10 (NKJV) – *Do you not know that the unrighteous will not inherit the kingdom of God? Do not be deceived. Neither fornicators, nor idolaters, nor adulterers, nor homosexuals, nor sodomites, nor thieves, nor covetous, nor drunkards, nor revilers, nor extortioners will inherit the kingdom of God.*

1 Corinthians 6:19 (NKJV) – *Or do you not know that your body is the temple of the Holy Spirit who is in you, whom you have from God, and you are not your own?*

1 Corinthians 10:13 (NKJV) – *No temptation has overtaken you except such as is common to man; but God is faithful, who will not allow you to be tempted beyond what you are able, but with the temptation will also make the way of escape, that you may be able to bear it.*

Ephesians 4:23-24 (NKJV) – *and be renewed in the spirit of your mind, and that you put on the new man which was created according to God, in true righteousness and holiness.*

Titus 1:7-8 (NKJV) – *For a bishop must be blameless, as a steward of God, not self-willed, not quick-tempered, not given to wine, not violent, not greedy for money, but hospitable, a lover of what is good, sober-minded, just, holy, self-controlled.*

1 Peter 5:7-8 (NKJV) – *Casting all your care upon Him, for He cares for you. Be sober, be vigilant; because your adversary the devil walks about like a roaring lion, seeking whom he may devour.*

1 John 4:4 (NKJV) – *You are of God, little children, and have overcome them, because He who is in you is greater than he who is in the world.*

1 John 5:5 (NKJV) – *Who is he who overcomes the world, but he who believes that Jesus is the Son of God?*

I DECLARE IN THE MIGHTY NAME OF KING JESUS:

⚔ Addiction does not rule me, my family, or my bloodline. You are my God and I have no other gods before You.

⚔ I have been set free from the bonds of addiction. Temptation has no hold over me.

⚔ You have made me an overcomer through the blood of Jesus, my Savior.

⚔ The devil may rage against me—he may tempt me—but the Lord has declared me victorious over the schemes of the enemy. Satan regrets the day he chose to mess with me.

⚔ I am filled with the fruit of the Spirit. Love and self-control belong to me.

⚔ Joy and peace are my trademarks. With the Holy Spirit, I can overcome any obstacle that springs up in my path.

⚔ God is clearing my path to my identity, purpose, and destiny. I am a sober-minded, powerful member of His Kingdom.

✝ No weapon of addiction fashioned against me shall prosper. You have given me a way out of every temptation because You are my strong tower. I am righteous and gladly run to You.

✝ The Holy Spirit is my Comforter and ever-present Help in time of need. He will convict and correct me swiftly and train me in righteousness.

✝ Because my desire is for You and Your Word, Jesus, I walk in complete victory over fleshly desires. My victory over addiction is complete because of Your finished work on the cross.

9

BATTLE CRY FOR VICTORY OVER GRIEF AND LOSS

The Lord is near to those who have a broken heart, and saves such as have a contrite [crushed] spirit. Many are the afflictions of the righteous, but the Lord delivers him out of them all (Psalm 34:18-19 NKJV).

Father, Your Word says You heal the brokenhearted and bind up their wounds (Psalm 147:3). Lord, my heart is broken and my spirit is crushed under the weight of grief and loss. Help me to be still and know that You are God (Psalm 46:10). You work all things for the good of those who love You and are called according to Your purposes (Romans 8:28). Help me to understand Your plan and praise You in the midst of this storm. Give me grace to find the confidence to overcome and embrace the new life You are bringing me.

Father, I know You are the God who understands loss. You sent the Word from Your home in Heaven to become the Son who was beaten and bruised for our transgressions. His blood was brutally spilled and His life taken so we could have redemption and restoration to You, Lord (Isaiah 53:4-5). How You must have grieved! How You must still grieve every time one of Your precious children rejects Your love. Father, Your empathy gives me comfort and hope. I hear Your words of comfort saying, "It's okay to weep, because you do not weep alone. I will be close with you until you can once again rejoice when I rejoice" (see Romans 12:15).

Help me to trade my sorrows for Your joy of the Lord, which is my strength now and always (Nehemiah 8:10). Comfort me in my affliction and give me life through the reading of Your Word (Psalm 119:50). I ask for beauty for ashes, the oil of joy for mourning, and the garment of praise for the spirit of heaviness that I might be called righteous and You may be glorified (Isaiah 61:3). Amen.

SCRIPTURES

Psalm 31:9-10 (NKJV) – *Have mercy on me, O Lord, for I am in trouble; my eye wastes away with grief, yes, my soul and my body! For my life is spent with grief, and my years with sighing; my strength fails because of my iniquity, and my bones waste away.*

Psalm 56:8 (NKJV) – *You number my wanderings; put my tears into Your bottle; are they not in Your book?*

Psalm 119:50 (NKJV) – *This is my comfort in my affliction, for Your word has given me life.*

Psalm 147:3 (NKJV) – *He heals the brokenhearted and binds up their wounds.*

Ecclesiastes 3:1-4 (NKJV) – *To everything there is a season, a time for every purpose under heaven: a time to be born, and a time to die; a time to plant, and a time to pluck what is planted; a time to kill, and a time to heal;*

a time to break down, and a time to build up; a time to weep, and a time to laugh; a time to mourn, and a time to dance.

Isaiah 53:4-5 (NKJV) – *Surely He has borne our griefs and carried our sorrows; yet we esteemed Him stricken, smitten by God, and afflicted. But He was wounded for our transgressions, He was bruised for our iniquities; the chastisement for our peace was upon Him, and by His stripes we are healed.*

Matthew 5:4 (NKJV) – *Blessed are those who mourn, for they shall be comforted.*

John 11:33 (NKJV) – *Therefore, when Jesus saw her weeping, and the Jews who came with her weeping, He groaned in the spirit and was troubled.*

John 14:1 (NKJV) – *Let not your heart be troubled; you believe in God, believe also in Me.*

John 16:33 (NKJV) – *These things I have spoken to you, that in Me you may have peace. In the world you will have tribulation; but be of good cheer. I have overcome the world.*

Romans 8:28 (NKJV) – *And we know that all things work together for good to those who love God, to those who are called according to His purpose.*

2 Corinthians 1:3 (NKJV) – *Blessed be the God and Father of our Lord Jesus Christ, the Father of mercies and God of all comfort.*

Revelation 21:4 (NKJV) – *And God will wipe away every tear from their eyes; there shall be no more death, nor* *sorrow, nor crying. There shall be no more pain, for the former things have passed away.*

I DECLARE VICTORY IN THE MIGHTY NAME OF KING JESUS:

- This is a time to mourn. It is okay to grieve and right that I should acknowledge the loss in my life.

- When the time to dance arrives, I will embrace it with a glad heart.

- I will trade my sorrows for joy for You have given me beauty for ashes, the oil of joy for mourning, and the garment of praise to replace the spirit of heaviness.

- I have tasted Your salvation and trust that Your plan for me is good.

- You work all things out for the good of those who love You. I can trust in Your redeeming power.

- "I would have lost heart, unless I had believed that I would see the goodness of God in the land of the living" (Psalm 27:13 NKJV).

- I have the faith to cast all my cares on Jesus because He cares for me.

- I rest in the promise of God's Word that You will never leave me nor forsake me. You, Lord, are in control.

- I walk by faith believing the Father to bring me good things in my life. I refuse to be afraid for my future because the Lord holds my future in His hands.

Because the Prince of Peace rules over me, I have peace in times of trouble. He has dominion over my heart, mind, and spirit. He is restoring my joy.

10

BATTLE CRY FOR REDEEMING TIME

You are so intimately aware of me, Lord. You read my heart like an open book and you know all the words I'm about to speak before I even start a sentence! You know every step I will take before my journey even begins. You've gone into my future to prepare the way, and in kindness you follow behind me to spare me from the harm of my past... (Psalm 139:3-5 The Passion Translation).

Jesus, You are the Creator of time. It is Your way of keeping everything from happening at once and is subject to You. I thank You that You created time for great acts of redemption. You know the end from the beginning (Isaiah 46:10)—You see it all from eternity. Lord, I ask that You go back into my timeline. Go back and redeem _____. I apply the blood of Jesus to this and declare a new beginning over that thing that has defined me. I proclaim redemption, restoration, and restitution over it and break off all unforgiveness, curses or iniquities that have sprung up as a result. Lord, I forgive and release those who have wronged me and ask You to cut out any bitter root in my heart.

Father, just as You stopped time for Joshua (Joshua 10:13) and turned back time for Hezekiah (Isaiah 38:8), I ask You to work all things in my past for the good of my present and future (Romans 8:28)—that I would walk out every step of the plan You have for my life. Please return to me the days the locust have eaten (Joel 2:25). Give me victory in this place of defeat and accelerate my purpose and destiny so I can glorify You.

Holy Spirit, teach me to number my days, that I might gain a heart of wisdom (Psalm 90:12). I want to weep when it's time to weep and laugh when it's time to laugh (Ecclesiastes 3:4). Mark me as upright that my end may be peace (Psalm 37:37). I ask all this in the mighty name of Jesus Christ. Amen.

SCRIPTURES

Genesis 1:1 (NKJV) – *In the beginning* **[time]** *God created the heavens* **[space]** *and the earth* **[matter].**

1 Chronicles 12:32 (NKJV) – *Of the sons of Issachar who had understanding of the times, to know what Israel ought to do....*

Psalm 139:7-10 (Passion Translation) – *Where could I go from your Spirit? Where could I run and hide from your face? If I go up to heaven* **[eternity],** *you're there! If I go down to the realm of the dead* **[eternity],** *you're there too! If I fly with wings into the shining dawn* **[the future],** *you're there! If I fly into the radiant sunset* **[the past],** *you're there waiting! Wherever I go, your hand will guide me; your strength will empower me.*

Ecclesiastes 3:1 (NKJV) – *To everything there is a season, a time for every purpose under heaven.*

Ecclesiastes 3:11 (NKJV) – *He has made everything beautiful in its time. Also He has put eternity in their hearts, except that no one can find out the work that God does from beginning to end.*

Joshua 10:13 (NKJV) – *So the sun stood still, and the moon stopped, till the people had revenge upon their enemies.*

Joel 2:23-25 (NKJV) – *...And He will cause the rain to come down for you—the former rain, and the latter rain in the first month. The threshing floors shall be full of wheat, and the vats shall overflow with new wine and oil. So I will restore to you the years that the swarming locust has eaten....*

Amos 9:13 (NKJV) – *...The plowman will overtake the reaper....*

Isaiah 1:18 (NKJV) – *"Come now, and let us reason together," says the Lord, "Though your sins are like scarlet, they shall be as white as snow; though they are red like crimson, they shall be as wool."*

Isaiah 38:8 (NKJV) – *"Behold, I will bring the shadow on the sundial, which has gone down with the sun on the sundial of Ahaz, ten degrees backward." So the sun returned ten degrees on the dial by which it had gone down.*

Isaiah 46:10 (NKJV) – *Declaring the end from the beginning, and from ancient times things that are not yet done, saying, "My counsel shall stand, and I will do all My pleasure."*

Daniel 2:21 (NKJV) – *And He changes the times and the seasons; He removes kings and raises up kings; He gives wisdom to the wise and knowledge to those who have understanding.*

Matthew 20:8 (NKJV) – *So when evening had come, the owner of the vineyard said to his steward, "Call the laborers and give them their wages, beginning with the last to the first."*

Matthew 24:22 (NKJV) – *And unless those days were shortened, no flesh would be saved; but for the elect's sake those days will be shortened.*

Acts 8:39-40 (NKJV) – *Now when they came up out of the water, the Spirit of the Lord caught Philip away, so that the eunuch saw him no more; and he went on his way rejoicing. But Philip was found at Azotus.*

Ephesians 5:16 (NKJV) – *Redeeming the time, because the days are evil.*

Revelation 1:8 (NKJV) – *"I am the Alpha and the Omega, the Beginning and the End," says the Lord, "who is and who was and who is to come, the Almighty."*

I DECLARE IN THE MIGHTY NAME OF KING JESUS:

I am forgiven and set free from my past! My sins were like a red cloth, staining my every moment. But You have turned back time. You have un-dyed that cloth and have made my today white as wool (Isaiah 1:18).

- I will not squander the gift You have given me. Time is a precious commodity and I will make the most of it.

- I declare supernatural provision. You are giving back the days the locusts have eaten in my relationships, my purpose, and my destiny.

- Supernatural understanding of times and seasons are mine. I have an Issachar anointing over my life that I would have a word in due season and bring blessing to all around me.

- Time is in Your hands and You will deliver me from my enemies (Psalm 31:15).

- The plowman of justice will overtake the reaper. You are restoring all the enemy has stolen.

- Accelerated timeframes are mine. What once took me years to accomplish will now take me weeks.

- Accelerated trajectory over my promise and prosperity. My goals will be reached in record time.

- I am the bride of Christ prepared for the marriage supper of the Lamb. As the return of Jesus draws near, You are speeding up time. The birth pains are accelerating. Behold, the Bridegroom comes!

- I am made "for such a time as this." I am the best of my bloodline, redeeming the time because the days are evil.

- I am in alignment for my assignment. I was born for such a time as this (Esther 4:14).

- My end shall be peace, for I walk upright in Your promises and power (Psalm 37:37).

11

BATTLE CRY FOR IDENTITY, PURPOSE, AND DESTINY

For we are His workmanship, created in Christ Jesus for good works, which God prepared beforehand that we should walk in them (Ephesians 2:10 NKJV).

Father God, when I think that I am not enough and I have fallen short, turn me back to Your Word that says I am Your servant, Your child, Your friend, and the bride of Christ. I thank You that the plans You have for me are for my good and prosperity. You will never harm me (Jeremiah 29:11). You know the end from the beginning and You see me as full and complete through Your Son, Jesus (Isaiah 46:10). Help me to see that too!

I will praise You for Your Word says I am fearfully and wonderfully made. You know me and my purpose completely (Psalm 139:14). I know Your thoughts for me are innumerable, Your grace is impenetrable, and Your love for me is immeasurable. Your redemption purchased my freedom from sin and death; and Your sacrifice, Jesus, secures me in Your family. You have indwelled me with your Holy Spirit as a deposit, guaranteeing my citizenship in Heaven (Philippians 3:20). Lord, bring to pass the incredible identity, purpose, and destiny You've created for me that I will walk out every step for Your glory. I ask all this in Jesus's mighty name. Amen.

SCRIPTURES

Jeremiah 1:5 (NKJV) – *Before I formed you in the womb I knew you; before you were born I sanctified you; I ordained you a prophet to the nations.*

Isaiah 55:11 (NKJV) – *So shall My word be that goes forth from My mouth; it shall not return to Me void, but it shall accomplish what I please, and it shall prosper in the thing for which I sent it.*

Proverbs 20:24 (NKJV) – *A man's steps are of the Lord; how then can a man understand his own way?*

Isaiah 49:16 (NKJV) – *See, I have inscribed you on the palms of My hands; Your walls are continually before Me.*

Psalm 37:37 (NKJV) – *Mark the blameless man, and observe the upright; for the future of that man is peace.*

Isaiah 54:5 (NKJV) – *For your Maker is your husband, the Lord of hosts is His name; and your Redeemer is the Holy One of Israel; He is called the God of the whole earth.*

John 1:12 (NKJV) – *But as many as received Him, to them He gave the right to become children of God, to those who believe in His name.*

Ephesians 1:5 (NKJV) – *Having predestined us to adoption as sons by Jesus Christ to Himself, according to the good pleasure of His will.*

1 Peter 2:9 (NKJV) – *But you are a chosen generation, a royal priesthood, a holy nation, His own special people, that you may proclaim the praises of Him who called you out of darkness into His marvelous light.*

Colossians 2:9-10 (NKJV) – *For in Him dwells all the fullness of the Godhead bodily; and you are complete in Him, who is the head of all principality and power.*

Romans 6:6 (NKJV) – *Knowing this, that our old man was crucified with Him, that the body of sin might be done away with, that we should no longer be slaves of sin.*

Genesis 1:27 (NKJV) – *So God created man in His own image; in the image of God He created him; male and female He created them.*

John 15:15 (NKJV) – *No longer do I call you servants, for a servant does not know what his master is doing; but I have called you friends, for all things that I heard from My Father I have made known to you.*

I DECLARE IN THE MIGHTY NAME OF KING JESUS:

- Your Word is truth and light. I replace the lies of the enemy with the truth of Your Word because Your banner over me is love.

- I was made to be full, complete, and victorious in You, Jesus. I am an overcomer!

- My works are committed to You, Lord. My thoughts are established in the identity You have given me.

- I am made in the image of Almighty God to be a priest and a king.

✝ You have filled me with insight, understanding, and knowledge. I have the mind of Christ and bring wise counsel into all situations.

✝ You have made me a winner, not a loser. Jesus has dominion in my life so my end shall be peace.

✝ I have committed my ways to You, Lord God. Carry out Your plan for my life!

✝ I am a joint-heir with Jesus and I have the mind of Christ. Greater things will I do.

✝ I am Your servant feeding the hungry, caring for the widow, loving the orphan, restoring the oppressed and preaching the Good News to the lost. I am no longer a slave to this world. You call me friend and I long for time in Your presence.

✝ I am the child of the Most High God. I have access to my Daddy day and night. I am welcome at His table.

✝ You are jealous for me. You are my Bridegroom and I am Your bride watching for Your glorious return. Come quickly, Jesus!

✝ I know all things work together for my good because I love God and am called according to His purpose.

12

BATTLE CRY FOR FINANCIAL FREEDOM

Give, and it will be given to you: good measure, pressed down, shaken together, and running over will be put into your bosom. For with the same measure that you use, it will be measured back to you (Luke 6:38 NKJV).

Father God, I praise You that You are Jehovah Jireh, my provider. All the cattle on a thousand hills is Yours (Psalm 50:10) and You have no lack. Everything I have is Yours because You have given it to me (Revelation 3:17). I thank You that You are changing my financial situation right now and I will no longer be a borrower but a lender to those in need. I praise You, Lord, that You are opening the heavens to send Your blessing on the work of my hands (Deuteronomy 28:12). Thank You for giving me richly all things to enjoy (1 Timothy 6:17). Let it be known this day that I serve You and no other, in Jesus's name.

SCRIPTURES

Proverbs 3:9-10 (NKJV) – *Honor the Lord with your possessions, and with the first fruits of all your increase; so your barns will be filled with plenty, and your vats will overflow with new wine.*

Hebrews 13:5 (NKJV) – *Let your conduct be without covetousness; be content with such things as you have. For He Himself has said, "I will never leave you nor forsake you."*

Malachi 3:10 (NKJV) – *"Bring all the tithes into the storehouse, that there may be food in My house, and try Me now in this," says the Lord of hosts, "If I will not open for you the windows of heaven and pour out for you such blessing that there will not be room enough to receive it."*

Matthew 6:21 (NKJV) – *Where your treasure is, there your heart will be also.*

Philippians 4:19 (NKJV) – *And my God shall supply all your need according to His riches in glory by Christ Jesus.*

Matthew 6:24 (NIV) – *No one can serve two masters. Either you will hate the one and love the other, or you will be devoted to the one and despise the other. You cannot serve both God and money.*

1 Timothy 6:10 (NIV) – *For the love of money is a root of all kinds of evil. Some people, eager for money, have wandered from the faith and pierced themselves with many griefs.*

Proverbs 10:4 (NIV) – *Lazy hands make for poverty, but diligent hands bring wealth.*

2 Corinthians 9:6-8 (NKJV) – *But this I say: He who sows sparingly will also reap sparingly, and he who sows bountifully will also reap bountifully. So let each one give as he purposes in his heart, not grudgingly or of necessity; for God loves a cheerful giver. And God is able to make all grace abound toward you, that you, always having all sufficiency in all things, may have an abundance for every good work.*

Deuteronomy 28:12 (NIV) – *The Lord will open the heavens, the storehouse of his bounty, to send rain on your land in season and to bless all the work of your hands. You will lend to many nations but will borrow from none.*

Proverbs 22:7 (NIV) – *The rich rule over the poor, and the borrower is servant to the lender.*

I DECLARE IN THE MIGHTY NAME OF KING JESUS:

- I am a supernatural giver and find joy in generosity. I can be trusted with worldly wealth and true riches.

- I am content with the things I have. You, God, supply all my needs according to Your riches in glory!

- I sow bountifully and will reap bountifully 30, 60, and 100-fold!

- My heart is with You, Lord, and so is my treasure.

- I am a lender, not a borrower. You are blessing the works of my hands.

- You have brought me streams in the desert and highways in the wilderness.

- Accelerated timelines and trajectory are mine! You are advancing me to new heights and obstacles are being removed.

- I am in alignment for my assignment. I am going after my destiny and You will bless me.

13

BATTLE CRY FOR HEALING

Surely He has borne our griefs and carried our sorrows; yet
we esteemed Him stricken, smitten by God, and afflicted. But
He was wounded for our transgressions, He was bruised for
our iniquities; the chastisement for our peace was upon Him,
and by His stripes we are healed (Isaiah 53:4-5 NKJV).

Lord, I thank You and I praise You that You hear my prayers. There is none like You. You are Jehovah Rapha (Exodus 15:26), my Healer. All healing comes from You. Lord, I thank You that it is by Your stripes that I am healed (Isaiah 53:4-5; 1 Peter 2:24). I look for the manifestation of my healing to break forth in Jesus's mighty name!

Your Word says not to be wise in my own eyes but to fear You and depart from evil; doing this will be health to my flesh and strength to my bones (Proverbs 3:8). So, Lord, I come to You humbly and ask You to help me to leave behind any way that is not of You. Lord, I ask You to search my heart and show me any offensive way within me that I may turn from it and toward You in repentance (Psalm 139:23-24).

Your name is above every name (Philippians 2:9-10) and every illness and disease must bow to the name of Jesus. Jesus redeemed me from the curse because He became a curse for me (Galatians 3:1-3). Thank You for Your blood that covers me. Your Word says that life is in the blood (Leviticus 17:11) and because Your blood covers me, Your life covers me and Your blood cleanses me of all sin (1 John 1:7). Thank You for delivering me out of all the afflictions coming against me (Psalm 34:17). I await Your perfect timing. Lord, increase my faith as I wait upon You. In Jesus's name I pray.

SCRIPTURES

1 Peter 2:24 (NKJV) – *Who Himself bore our sins in His own body on the tree, that we, having died to sins, might live for righteousness—by whose stripes you were healed.*

Proverbs 4:20-22 (NIV) – *My son, pay attention to what I say; turn your ear to my words. Do not let them out of your sight, keep them within your heart; for they are life to those who find them and health to one's whole body.*

3 John 1:2 (NKJV) – *Beloved, I pray that you may prosper in all things and be in health, just as your soul prospers.*

Jeremiah 17:14 (NIV) – *Heal me, Lord, and I will be healed; save me and I will be saved, for you are the one I praise.*

James 5:14-16 (NKJV) – *Is anyone among you sick? Let him call for the elders of the church, and let them pray over him, anointing him with oil in the name of the Lord. And the prayer of faith will save the sick, and the Lord will raise him up. And if he has committed sins, he will be forgiven. Confess your trespasses to one another, and* *pray for one another, that you may be healed. The effective, fervent prayer of a righteous man avails much.*

Jeremiah 30:17 (NKJV) – *"For I will restore health to you and heal you of your wounds," says the Lord....*

Jeremiah 33:6 (NIV) – *Nevertheless, I will bring health and healing to it; I will heal my people and will let them enjoy abundant peace and security.*

Psalm 34:19 (NKJV) – *Many are the afflictions of the righteous, but the Lord delivers him out of them all.*

I DECLARE IN THE MIGHTY NAME OF KING JESUS:

- I am an overcomer because of Your blood and the word of my testimony (Revelation 12:11).

- No weapon formed against me shall prosper and every tongue that rises against me in judgment shall be condemned! This is my heritage as a servant of the Lord from whom my righteousness comes (Isaiah 54:17).

- All curses over my life are broken right now in the name of Jesus!

- Any negative report spoken over me is null and void and I come out of agreement with it in Jesus's mighty name!

- Complete physical and emotional healing in my life. You have given me abundant peace and security (Jeremiah 33:6).

✝ That You sustain me on my sickbed and restore me from my bed of illness (Psalm 41:3).

✝ The binding up and the healing of the broken places in my life in Jesus's name (Isaiah 61:1).

✝ That by Your blood I am made whole and by Your stripes I am healed (1 Peter 2:24).

✝ You, Jesus, paid the price for my healing. I am whole and I walk in the knowledge of Your love and sacrifice. I am healed in Your name!

14

BATTLE CRY FOR MARRIAGE AND COVENANT

The Lord God said, "It is not good for the man to be alone. I will make a helper suitable for him." ...The man said, "This is now bone of my bones and flesh of my flesh; she shall be called 'woman,' for she was taken out of man." That is why a man leaves his father and mother and is united to his wife, and they become one flesh (Genesis 2:18,23-24 NIV).

Father God, I thank You for the covenant You have made with me. I know I am Your beloved bride. I also thank You for the covenant of marriage You have given me with my spouse. We are a picture of Your love and unity with the Son and the Spirit. Just as You will never leave us nor forsake us, Lord, my pledge is to love and keep my spouse until death separates us.

Father, I ask You to pour identity, purpose, and destiny into us, that together we would walk out every step You've planned for us joyfully and under the direction of Your Holy Spirit. Give us wisdom and strength to navigate the calm and weather the storms so our marriage will be a testimony of You.

Jesus, Your blood has paid for the forgiveness of our sins. I pray You give me the humility and wisdom to forgive the things I need to forgive in my spouse and to ask forgiveness when I am the one who fails. Do not let the sun go down on any anger we may be holding. I renounce any stronghold of bitterness that might be growing between us, in Jesus's name.

Lord, give us eyes to see and ears to hear not only You but one another. Give us kind, supporting words to lead and guide each other. Help us love and respect each other no matter the season. Jesus, cause us to pray for one another and to seek You first in our marriage each day. Bring us from deep unto deep and spark an intimacy between us that both fulfills and protects. What You have brought together, no one or scheme of the enemy can separate. You are our center, our Beloved, and we are Yours. Amen.

SCRIPTURES

Proverbs 5:18-19 (NKJV) – *Let your fountain be blessed, and rejoice with the wife of your youth...and always be enraptured with her love.*

Proverbs 12:4 (NKJV) – *An excellent wife is the crown of her husband, but she who causes shame is like rottenness in his bones.*

Proverbs 18:22 (NKJV) – *He who finds a wife finds a good thing, and obtains favor from the Lord.*

Ecclesiastes 4:9-11 (NKJV) – *Two are better than one, because they have a good reward for their labor. For if they fall, one will lift up his companion. But woe to him who is alone when he falls, for he has no one to help him* *up. Again, if two lie down together, they will keep warm; but how can one be warm alone?*

Matthew 19:4-6 (NKJV) – *And He answered and said to them, "Have you not read that He who made them at the beginning 'made them male and female,' and said, 'For this reason a man shall leave his father and mother and be joined to his wife, and the two shall become one flesh'? So then, they are no longer two but one flesh. Therefore what God has joined together, let not man separate."*

Romans 12:2 (NKJV) – *And do not be conformed to this world, but be transformed by the renewing of your mind, that you may prove what is that good and acceptable and perfect will of God.*

2 Corinthians 6:14 (NKJV) – *Do not be unequally yoked together with unbelievers. For what fellowship has righteousness with lawlessness? And what communion has light with darkness?*

Ephesians 5:22-24 (NKJV) – *Wives, submit to your own husbands, as to the Lord. For the husband is head of the wife, as also Christ is head of the church; and He is the Savior of the body. Therefore, just as the church is subject to Christ, so let the wives be to their own husbands in everything.*

Ephesians 5:25,28,33 (NKJV) – *Husbands, love your wives, just as Christ also loved the church and gave Himself for her.... So husbands ought to love their own wives as their own bodies; he who loves his wife loves himself. ...Nevertheless let each one of you in particular* *so love his own wife as himself, and let the wife see that she respects her husband.*

1 Thessalonians 4:3-5 (NKJV) – *For this is the will of God, your sanctification: that you should abstain from sexual immorality; that each of you should know how to possess his own vessel in sanctification and honor, not in passion of lust, like the Gentiles who do not know God.*

Hebrews 13:4 (NKJV) – *Marriage is honorable among all, and the bed undefiled; but fornicators and adulterers God will judge.*

1 Peter 3:1 (NKJV) – *Wives, likewise, be submissive to your own husbands, that even if some do not obey the word, they, without a word, may be won by the conduct of their wives.*

1 Peter 3:7 (NKJV) – *Husbands, likewise, dwell with them with understanding, giving honor to the wife, as to the weaker vessel, and as being heirs together of the grace of life, that your prayers may not be hindered.*

I DECLARE IN THE MIGHTY NAME OF KING JESUS:

✝ You are the God of covenant. Because You have kept Your covenant with me, I will joyfully keep my marriage covenant.

✝ Jesus, You are my Beloved and I am Yours. The relationship I have with You will strengthen and guide me in my relationship with my spouse.

✝ I pray daily for the encouragement, strengthening, and comfort of my mate.

✝ My lips will not criticize or berate my beloved. I am my spouse's support in times of trouble and I will encourage my mate to advance in every way.

✝ I am proud of the mate You have given me, Lord. You know my needs and You gave me my perfect match. Together, we will accomplish much for the Kingdom.

✝ I will selflessly serve and put my mate's needs and best interests before my own.

✝ I commit to love my spouse like Christ loved the Church. He willingly laid down His own desires to bring us life. I will lay down any selfish desire I have for the good of our marriage.

✝ I speak only life over my beloved and will build up my mate in word and deed.

✝ I am slow to anger, quick to forgive and will not let the sun go down on my anger. I will not let my beloved lose hope in my love.

✝ I respect my spouse and keep myself only for my spouse. I will never leave nor forsake my beloved.

✝ I will love my spouse selflessly through debt and riches, sickness and health, trial and test.

✝ It is my priority to support and encourage my mate to fulfill their identity, purpose, and destiny in Jesus.

✝ We will see the goodness of God in our marriage because we stand in unity with Jesus, our Creator.

15

BATTLE CRY FOR PROSPERITY IN BUSINESS

And I have filled him with the Spirit of God, in wisdom, in understanding, in knowledge, and in all manner of workmanship, to design artistic works, to work in gold, in silver, in bronze, in cutting jewels for setting, in carving wood, and to work in all manner of workmanship (Exodus 31:3-5 NKJV).

Lord, I come today thanking You for the enduring riches, honor, and righteousness You have blessed me with (Proverbs 8:18). I know You only give the power to gain wealth because You have established Your covenant with me and my generations (Deuteronomy 8:18). You keep Your promises. Father, I seek Your forgiveness for the times I've failed by not seeking Your will and plan. Like Joshua, I stretch out my spear toward that place of stumbling and proclaim victory over defeat and restoration for what was lost (Joshua 8:18).

Jesus, I thank You for the wise counsel You have provided and ask You to continue to bring me mentors of great understanding to move my ventures forward for the Kingdom (Ezra 8:18). I declare supernatural provision and abundance over my work, that non-believers would invest in Kingdom projects (2 Chronicles 8:18). Let me and my business be for signs, miracles, and wonders—that the lost would be found through the work of my hands (Isaiah 8:18). Lord, I hear Your calling on my life and ask You to increase my territory and capacity (Luke 8:18).

Holy Spirit, You have my ear. I am listening to Your leading (Psalm 81:8). I know Your glory will be revealed in me and my business in this season (Romans 8:18). You have taken me from the sleep of idleness, touched me and stood me upright (Daniel 8:18) to do good works that You planned for me long before I was born. I am so grateful that You have spoken to me concerning my business ventures (Zechariah 8:18) and given me integrity, wisdom, and a heart to serve like Jesus. I proclaim any hardships I encounter building this Kingdom asset are not worthy to be compared to the glory You are revealing in me through this purpose (Romans 8:18). You are good, and I commit my ways to You in all I do. Amen.

SCRIPTURES

CALLING & PURPOSE

Genesis 2:15 (NKJV) – *Then the Lord God took the man and put him in the garden of Eden to tend and keep it.*

Exodus 35:35 (NKJV) – *He has filled them with skill to do all manner of work of the engraver and the designer and the tapestry maker, in blue, purple, and scarlet thread, and fine linen, and of the weaver—those who do every work and those who design artistic works.*

Luke 19:13 (NKJV) – *So he called ten of his servants, delivered to them ten minas, and said to them, "Do business till I come."*

HONESTY & INTEGRITY

Job 31:6 (NKJV) – *Let me be weighed on honest scales, that God may know my integrity.*

Psalm 112:5 (NKJV) – *A good man deals graciously and lends; he will guide his affairs with discretion.*

Proverbs 11:1 (NKJV) – *Dishonest scales are an abomination to the Lord, but a just weight is His delight.*

Proverbs 22:16 (NKJV) – *He who oppresses the poor to increase his riches, and he who gives to the rich, will surely come to poverty.*

SKILLS & TALENTS

Proverbs 22:29 (NKJV) – *Do you see a man who excels in his work? He will stand before kings; he will not stand before unknown [obscure] men.*

Ephesians 2:10 (NKJV) – *For we are His workmanship, created in Christ Jesus for good works, which God prepared beforehand that we should walk in them.*

1 Corinthians 12:4-6 (NKJV) – *There are diversities of gifts, but the same Spirit. There are differences of ministries, but the same Lord. And there are diversities of activities, but it is the same God who works all in all.*

AVOIDING EASY WEALTH & SCHEMES

Proverbs 13:11 (NKJV) – *Wealth gained by dishonesty will be diminished, but he who gathers by labor will increase.*

Proverbs 14:23 (NKJV) – *In all labor there is profit, but idle chatter leads only to poverty.*

Proverbs 21:5 (NKJV) – *The plans of the diligent lead surely to plenty, but those of everyone who is hasty, surely to poverty.*

SERVING OTHERS

Proverbs 27:18 (NKJV) – *Whoever keeps the fig tree will eat its fruit; so he who waits on his master will be honored.*

Colossians 3:23-24 (NKJV) – *And whatever you do, do it heartily, as to the Lord and not to men, knowing that from the Lord you will receive the reward of the inheritance; for you serve the Lord Christ.*

LEADERSHIP & WORK ETHIC

Matthew 20:26 (NKJV) – *Yet it shall not be so among you; but whoever desires to become great among you, let him be your servant.*

Proverbs 13:4 (NKJV) – *The soul of a lazy man desires, and has nothing; but the soul of the diligent shall be made rich.*

Proverbs 19:15 (NKJV) – *Laziness casts one into a deep sleep, and an idle person will suffer hunger.*

Ecclesiastes 9:10 (NKJV) – *Whatever your hand finds to do, do it with your might; for there is no work or device or knowledge or wisdom in the grave where you are going.*

Success in Business

Deuteronomy 8:18 (NKJV) – *And you shall remember the Lord your God, for it is He who gives you power to get wealth, that He may establish His covenant which He swore to your fathers, as it is this day.*

Proverbs 23:4 (NKJV) – *Do not overwork to be rich; because of your own understanding, cease!*

Nehemiah 6:9 (NKJV) – *For they all were trying to make us afraid, saying, "Their hands will be weakened in the work, and it will not be done." Now therefore, O God, strengthen my hands.*

Mark 8:36 (NKJV) – *For what will it profit a man if he gains the whole world, and loses his own soul?*

Business Strategy

1 Chronicles 12:32 (NKJV) – *of the sons of Issachar who had understanding of the times, to know what Israel ought to do, their chiefs were two hundred; and all their brethren were at their command.*

Ecclesiastes 3:1-2 (NKJV) – *To everything there is a season, a time for every purpose under heaven…a time to plant, and a time to pluck what is planted.*

Proverbs 20:18 (NKJV) – *Plans are established by counsel; by wise counsel wage war.*

Proverbs 16:3 (NKJV) – *Commit your works to the Lord, and your thoughts will be established.*

Proverbs 14:15 (NKJV) – *The simple believes every word, but the prudent considers well his steps.*

I DECLARE IN THE MIGHTY NAME OF KING JESUS:

- I am a supernatural giver and find joy in generosity. I can be trusted with worldly wealth and true riches.

- I am content with the things I have. You, God, supply all my needs according to Your riches in glory!

- I sow bountifully and will reap bountifully—30, 60, and 100-fold! My heart is with You, Lord, and so is my treasure.

- I am a lender, not a borrower. You are blessing the works of my hands through my business ventures.

- I seek Your wisdom and will before making all decisions. You give me insight and integrity in all I do.

- You have given me next-level relationships for financial and Kingdom abundance. I gladly walk in wise counsel.

† You have brought me streams in the desert and highways in the wilderness. Prosperity and success are Your gifts to me to bless those around me.

† Accelerated timelines and trajectory are mine! You are advancing me to new heights and obstacles are being removed.

† I am in alignment for my assignment. I am a merchant pouring the marketplace into the ministry.

† I am going after my destiny and You will bless me for my faithfulness by allowing me to bring real life and FREEDOM to others.

† New beginnings and abundant life are mine through Your 8:18 Scriptures.

† The lines fall unto me in pleasant places. Logistical miracles belong to me.

† Because I follow You and honor You with my identity, purpose, and destiny, Your Kingdom will come and Your will is being done on this earth as it is in Your Kingdom.

16

BATTLE CRY FOR SONSHIP AND BELONGING

And because you are sons, God has sent forth the Spirit of His Son into your hearts, crying out, "Abba, Father!" Therefore you are no longer a slave but a son, and if a son, then an heir of God through Christ (Galatians 4:6-7 NKJV).

Father God, You know everything there is to know about me—every movement of my heart and soul. You understand my every thought before it enters my mind. I thank You that You are so intimately aware of me that You read my heart like an open book. You know every word I'm about to speak before I even start a sentence and every step I'll take before my journey begins. I am Your beloved child and You've gone into my future to prepare a purpose and destiny for me. In kindness, You follow behind me to redeem my past hurts and failures. There is no place I can hide from Your presence because You love me completely and enjoy my company (Psalm 139).

Your Word says that You delight in me (Psalm 147:11). You are never disappointed in my failures. Because You love me, You convict me, correct me, and train me in righteousness (2 Timothy 3:16). You think good thoughts toward me. I have called on Your name and sought You with my whole heart. You have led me out of the captivity of sin and death (Jeremiah 29:11-14). You have put Your Holy Spirit in me as a deposit, guaranteeing we will be together for eternity (Ephesians 1:14). Any voice or thought telling me I am an orphan is a liar. I am loved no matter my circumstance. I am Yours even when I feel alone. Help me to stand upright so that my end shall be peace (Psalm 37:37). I will hear You say, "This is My Son in whom I am well pleased" when I meet You in Heaven. Amen.

SCRIPTURES

Matthew 3:17 (NKJV) – *And suddenly a voice came from heaven, saying, "This is My beloved Son, in whom I am well pleased."*

John 1:12 (NKJV) – *But as many as received Him, to them He gave the right to become children of God, to those who believe in His name:*

Ephesians 1:5-6 (NKJV) – *Having predestined us to adoption as sons by Jesus Christ to Himself, according to the good pleasure of His will to the praise of the glory of His grace, by which He made us accepted in the Beloved.*

Romans 8:15-16 (NKJV) – *For you did not receive the spirit of bondage again to fear, but you received the Spirit of adoption by whom we cry out, "Abba, Father." The Spirit Himself bears witness with our spirit that we are children of God.*

1 John 3:1 (NKJV) – *Behold what manner of love the Father has bestowed on us, that we should be called* *children of God! Therefore the world does not know us, because it did not know Him.*

Romans 8:23 (NKJV) – *Not only that, but we also who have the firstfruits of the Spirit, even we ourselves groan within ourselves, eagerly waiting for the adoption, the redemption of our body.*

Galatians 3:26 (NKJV) – *For you are all sons of God through faith in Christ Jesus.*

Romans 8:14 (NKJV) – *For as many as are led by the Spirit of God, these are sons of God.*

Galatians 4:4-5 (NKJV) – *But when the fullness of the time had come, God sent forth His Son, born of a woman, born under the law, to redeem those who were under the law, that we might receive the adoption as sons.*

I DECLARE IN THE MIGHTY NAME OF KING JESUS:

- You have never left me nor forsaken Me. You are faithful and I will trust in You (Hebrews 13:5).

- I am not an orphan and I will not partner with any power or principality that says I am Fatherless.

- You will never abandon me because You keep Your covenants. I am adopted into Your family and You have a place for me in Your Kingdom (Romans 8:15-16).

✝ Even when I cannot hear Your voice or feel Your presence, You are here. I will not trust my feelings but have faith in Your Word (Jeremiah 17:9).

✝ I have all Your time and all Your attention because Your love is limitless (Ephesians 3:17-19). I will not mistake exclusiveness with loneliness.

✝ The resources of Heaven are mine. When I ask for a fish, You will not give me a stone because You are good (Luke 11:11-13).

✝ I am a joint heir with Jesus. I have a rich inheritance for the Kingdom (Romans 8:17).

✝ A thousand of my generations will be blessed because You have chosen me. I keep Your commands (Deuteronomy 7:9; Exodus 20:6).

✝ You prepare a table for me in the presence of my enemies. You call me family in the midst of defeat and anoint my head with the oil of healing. My life overflows with blessings (Psalm 23:5).

✝ You call me the head and not the tail; above and not beneath because You are a good Father (Deuteronomy 28:13). You never lie (Numbers 23:19).

✝ I am highly favored. You hear my prayers and allow them to influence Heaven. You give me authority to trample the serpent in Your name (Luke 10:19).

✝ You have not given me a spirit of fear, but of power, love, and a sound mind (2 Timothy 1:7). I can do all things through You because You strengthen me (Philippians 4:13).

17

BATTLE CRY FOR VICTORY OVER OFFENSE

Then He said to the disciples, "It is impossible that no offenses should come, but woe to him through whom they do come! ...Take heed to yourselves. If your brother sins against you, rebuke him; and if he repents, forgive him. And if he sins against you seven times in a day, and seven times in a day returns to you, saying, 'I repent,' you shall forgive him" (Luke 17:1,3-4 NKJV).

Father, I know offense is a choice and I come before You asking forgiveness for choosing offense over love. It is a trap that divides and destroys all who partner with it. Break the chains of suspicion, envy, pride, and bitterness that have enslaved me. I forgive those who have offended me and ask that You, Lord, pardon me for the times I've taken the bait of the enemy against You, my brothers and sisters. Give me a ministry of reconciliation. Where offense once thrived, let grace be much more plentiful.

Lord, I know that to be offended is to be "off-ended"—that I am not able to stand or walk straight. My testimony has been compromised, and I ask that You restore me. Deliver me from this evil and give me the patience and love to turn the other cheek when offenses come my way. Light my path so I can avoid the snares set before me. Do not let my words or actions be stumbling blocks that harden hearts, enslave others, or cause division. Jesus, let me be a peacemaker for You!

Holy Spirit, bind up any wound in me caused by offense. Heal my heart and mind so I can love others into the Kingdom. I understand that the Gospel of Jesus is offensive. It divides light from dark, good from evil. Lord, make me an instrument of Your peace so I can win the lost and rebellious for You. I ask this in Jesus's name. Amen.

SCRIPTURES

Job 16:10 (NKJV) – *They gape at me with their mouth, they strike me reproachfully on the cheek, they gather together against me.*

Psalm 15:3 (NKJV) – *He who does not backbite with his tongue, nor does evil to his neighbor, nor does he take up a reproach against his friend.*

Psalm 55:12-14 (NKJV) – *For it is not an enemy who reproaches me; then I could bear it. Nor is it one who hates me who has exalted himself against me; then I could hide from him. But it was you, a man my equal, my companion and my acquaintance. We took sweet counsel together, and walked to the house of God in the throng.*

Proverbs 18:19 (NKJV) – *A brother offended is harder to win than a strong city, and contentions are like the bars of a castle.*

Ecclesiastes 10:4 (NKJV) – *If the spirit of the ruler rises against you, do not leave your post; for conciliation pacifies great offenses.*

Matthew 24:10 (NKJV) – *And then many will be offended, will betray one another, and will hate one another.*

Acts 24:16 (NKJV) – *...I myself always strive to have a conscience without offense toward God and men.*

Romans 5:20 (NKJV) – *Moreover the law entered that the offense might abound. But where sin abounded, grace abounded much more,*

Romans 16:17 (NKJV) – *Now I urge you, brethren, note those who cause divisions and offenses, contrary to the doctrine which you learned, and avoid them.*

1 Corinthians 10:32 (NKJV) – *Give no offense, either to the Jews or to the Greeks or to the church of God.*

2 Corinthians 6:3 (NKJV) – *We give no offense in anything, that our ministry may not be blamed.*

2 Timothy 2:24-26 (NKJV) – *And a servant of the Lord must not quarrel but be gentle to all, able to teach, patient, in humility correcting those who are in opposition, if God perhaps will grant them repentance, so that they may know the truth and that they may come to their senses and escape the snare of the devil, having been taken captive by him to do his will.*

Isaiah 8:14 (NKJV) – *He [the Lord] will be as a sanctuary, but a stone of stumbling and a rock of offense to both the houses of Israel, as a trap and a snare to the inhabitants of Jerusalem.*

Romans 9:33 (NKJV) – *As it is written: "Behold, I lay in Zion a stumbling stone and rock of offense, and whoever believes on Him will not be put to shame."*

Luke 7:23 (NKJV) – *And blessed is he who is not offended because of Me.*

I DECLARE IN THE MIGHTY NAME OF KING JESUS:

† I repent of the stumbling block of offense. The spirit of discernment is revealing the traps set before me so I can avoid this pit.

† I refuse to partner with offense by being slow to anger, abounding in love, and quick to forgive those who have trespassed against me.

† When offenses come my way, I call on the Holy Spirit to give me peace and patience, that anger or jealousy would not rise up and devour me.

† I renounce all bitterness against those who have offended me and reject any envy I may feel toward others. These are a trap that will kill my testimony and steal my peace.

† I have the gift of discernment. I avoid division in my family and church by the counsel of the Holy Spirit.

† I declare the healing love of Yeshua over the wounds in my life caused by offense.

ɫ I will not be a stumbling block to others by spreading offense. Instead, I will prophesy for the strengthening, encouragement, and comfort of those around me.

ɫ I bring reconciliation into offensive situations. I will not pick up the offenses of others and will provide wise counsel against offense when those around me air their grievances.

ɫ I am dead to pride. My defender is Jesus and He will take up a standard for me. The battle belongs to Him.

ɫ Both my spiritual and natural eyes are opened to offense. I recognize the enemy's crafty attempt to disguise offense as godliness and avoid the trap.

18

BATTLE CRY FOR VICTORY OVER THE POVERTY SPIRIT

Restore now to them, even this day, their lands, their vineyards, their olive groves, and their houses, also a hundredth of the money and the grain, the new wine and the oil, that you have charged them (Nehemiah 5:11 NKJV).

King Jesus, You have made me mighty for the pulling down of strongholds, the casting down of evil imaginations and every high thing that exalts itself against the knowledge of You (2 Corinthians 10:4-5). I pull down the stronghold of poverty that I have partnered with and cast down the spirit of fear and the evil imagination that God wants me to be poor. It is a lie from the pit of hell. Jesus, let abundance be made manifest in my thinking, relationships, and finances. Tear down the works of the enemy (1 John 3:8) and every hidden offense in my heart that is keeping me from abundance throughout my life.

Father God, open Your good treasure to me. Pour out rain in its season and bless the works of my hands that I will lend and not borrow (Deuteronomy 28:12). Lord, bless me indeed and enlarge my territory for You—my sphere of influence for Your Kingdom (1 Chronicles 4:10) that many would be brought to repentance through Your abundance in my life. Because You love me, You prepare a table before me in the presence of my enemies. You anoint my head with the oil of health. Because of Your loving provision, my cup of joy runs over (Psalm 23:5). I have great worth in Your Kingdom!

Holy Spirit, change my heart. I choose to be a cheerful giver (2 Corinthians 9:7) bringing my tithe eagerly to Your storehouses (Malachi 3:10). I claim the promise that You will return to me with "good measure, pressed down, and shaken together and running over" (Luke 6:38). You promise to pay back to me more than I have given to those in need (Proverbs 19:17). Just as Elijah and Elisha blessed the widows with abundant oil in times of need, Lord, resource me with the oil of Heaven.

My heart is so grateful, Lord. I thank You for supplying all I need according to Your riches in glory (Philippians 4:19). I pray this in the mighty name of Jesus. Amen.

SCRIPTURES

Deuteronomy 8:18 (NKJV) – *And you shall remember the Lord your God, for it is He who gives you power to get wealth, that He may establish His covenant which He swore to your fathers, as it is this day.*

Proverbs 20:13 (NKJV) – *Do not love sleep, lest you come to poverty; open your eyes, and you will be satisfied with bread.*

Proverbs 22:7 (NKJV) – *The rich rules over the poor, and the borrower is servant to the lender.*

Ezekiel 16:49 (NKJV) – *Look, this was the iniquity of your sister Sodom: She and her daughter had pride, fullness* of food, and abundance of idleness; neither did she strengthen the hand of the poor and needy.

Malachi 3:10 (NKJV) – "Bring all the tithes into the storehouse, that there may be food in My house, and try Me now in this," says the Lord of hosts, "If I will not open for you the windows of heaven and pour out for you such blessing that there will not be room enough to receive it."

Matthew 6:31 (NKJV) – Therefore do not worry, saying, "What shall we eat?" or "What shall we drink?" or "What shall we wear?"

Matthew 6:33 (NKJV) – But seek first the kingdom of God and His righteousness, and all these things shall be added to you.

Luke 6:38 (NKJV) – Give, and it will be given to you: good measure, pressed down, shaken together, and running over will be put into your bosom. For with the same measure that you use, it will be measured back to you.

John 10:10 (NKJV) – The thief does not come except to steal, and to kill, and to destroy. I have come that they may have life, and that they may have it more abundantly.

John 15:5 (NKJV) – I am the vine, you are the branches. He who abides in Me, and I in him, bears much fruit; for without Me you can do nothing.

Philippians 4:11-12 (NKJV) – Not that I speak in regard to need, for I have learned in whatever state I am, to be content: I know how to be abased, and I know how to abound. Everywhere and in all things I have learned *both to be full and to be hungry, both to abound and to suffer need.*

3 John 1:2 (NKJV) – *Beloved, I pray that you may prosper in all things and be in health, just as your soul prospers.*

I DECLARE IN THE MIGHTY NAME OF KING JESUS:

- You are the God of abundance. You did not create me to live in lack but to be blessed with Your riches in glory. You truly love me, King Jesus!

- I come out of agreement with the spirit and principality of poverty. The devil is a liar and I proclaim new wine and oil overflowing in every aspect of my life.

- Never again will I confess lack. I am not ignorant of the enemy's schemes. I resist the devil because God promises that the devil will flee from me (James 4:7).

- You, Lord, are opening the windows of Heaven to me. I have been rewarded with increase and plenty. You restore the days the locusts have eaten (Joel 2:25) and repay what was stolen by the enemy.

- I repent of fear and worry. You have given me good gifts because You are a good Father who loves me and answers my prayers.

- Your word says riches and honor are with me— enduring riches and righteousness (Proverbs 8:18). I embrace this promise!

✝ It is You, Lord, who gives me the power to gain wealth that You may establish Your covenant which You swore to My fathers (Deuteronomy 8:18). You are blessing me 30, 60, and 100-fold so that I can be a blessing.

✝ You are the lifter of my head. I repent of financial sin.

✝ I break off the spirit of offense. Offense says it's not fair that others have more than me. When I am offended, I am saying I am powerless, which is partnering with poverty. This is a lie of the enemy and I repent of offense.

19

BATTLE CRY FOR REVERSE, REDEMPTION, AND RESTITUTION

The thief does not come except to steal, and to kill, and to destroy. I have come that they may have life, and that they may have it more abundantly (John 10:10 NKJV).

Lord Jesus, redemption is a big deal to You. You are the Author and Finisher of my faith (Hebrews 12:2) and You have written my story in Your redeeming blood (Hebrews 10:7). I thank You for the salvation and eternal life Your redemption brings. The promise of Heaven with You is my greatest treasure, and redemption Your greatest gift.

Because redemption is the cornerstone of Your character, I ask for justice here on earth. Lord, I ask You to reverse the curse of the enemy upon me. Restore to me all he has taken. He has stolen my time, my money, my relationships, opportunities, future, and so much more. Your Word says he is a liar and a thief who comes to "steal, kill and destroy" (John 10:10). I come out of agreement with any curse I have brought on myself or permission I have given the enemy to come against me. I ask Your forgiveness and restoration over those places in my life, Father God.

I stand on that same John 10:10 word that says You, Jesus, "have come that they may have life, and that they may have it more abundantly." On this promise, I declare the thief has been caught and ask You, the Righteous Judge, to find the "accuser of the brethren, who accuses them before our God day and night" guilty of theft and "cast down" this liar (Revelation 12:10). Jesus, I ask You as my Defense (Psalm 18:2) and Your Holy Spirit as my Counselor (John 14:26), to find me innocent based on Your redemption and sacrifice. Restore to me the days the locusts have eaten (Joel 2:25) and reverse the curses on my family, finances, friendships, and every bit of my identity, purpose, and destiny with seven-fold restitution (Proverbs 6:31). Thank You for hearing my cry and I look forward to seeing Your redemption and restitution pour out in my life. Amen.

SCRIPTURES

Ephesians 1:7 (NKJV) – *In Him we have redemption through His blood, the forgiveness of sins, according to the riches of His grace.*

Isaiah 44:22 (NKJV) – *I have blotted out, like a thick cloud, your transgressions, and like a cloud, your sins. Return to Me, for I have redeemed you.*

1 Peter 1:18-19 (NKJV) – *Knowing that you were not redeemed with corruptible things, like silver or gold, from your aimless conduct received by tradition from your fathers, but with the precious blood of Christ, as of a lamb without blemish and without spot.*

Psalm 51:12 (NKJV) – *Restore to me the joy of Your salvation, and uphold me by Your generous Spirit.*

Job 42:10 (NKJV) – *And the Lord restored Job's losses when he prayed for his friends. Indeed the Lord gave Job twice as much as he had before.*

Isaiah 61:3 (NKJV) – *To console those who mourn in Zion, to give them beauty for ashes, the oil of joy for mourning, the garment of praise for the spirit of heaviness; that they may be called trees of righteousness, the planting of the Lord, that He may be glorified.*

Jeremiah 30:17-18 (NKJV) – *"For I will restore health to you and heal you of your wounds," says the Lord, "Because they called you an outcast saying: 'This is Zion; no one seeks her.' Thus says the Lord: 'Behold, I will bring back the captivity of Jacob's tents, and have mercy on his dwelling places; the city shall be built upon its own mound, and the palace shall remain according to its own plan.'"*

Deuteronomy 6:10-11 (NKJV) – *So it shall be, when the Lord your God brings you into the land of which He swore to your fathers, to Abraham, Isaac, and Jacob, to give you large and beautiful cities which you did not build, houses full of all good things, which you did not fill, hewn-out wells which you did not dig, vineyards and olive trees which you did not plant—when you have eaten and are full.*

I DECLARE IN THE MIGHTY NAME OF KING JESUS:

✟ The devil is a liar and I come out of agreement with any lie he has told about me. I cast down his accusations and trample that snake under my feet by Your Word (Luke 10:19).

✟ I use the Matthew 16:19 authority given me by King Jesus to bind the lies and schemes of the devil here on earth as they are bound in Heaven. I loose truth, redemption, and restitution over the following areas of my life _____ .

✟ The Isaiah 22:22 key of the house of David has been laid upon my shoulders. I am opening doors to Heaven's justice that no one can shut and am, right now, shutting the door to the schemes of the enemy. He can no longer steal from me.

✟ By Romans 3:4, God is true, and every human a liar so that I may be proven right when I speak and prevail when I judge.

✟ Family, friendships, and all broken relationships are being restored for the glory of the Kingdom.

✟ Finances, fortunes, and my future are being redeemed by the blood of Jesus. He is going into the storehouse of hell and returning all the enemy has taken.

✟ Heaven's original intent for my life is being redeemed and restored (Psalm 139:16-18). Every lie from the pit of hell is being washed away so I will walk in the fullness of my Kingdom calling.

⚔ Jesus is the Righteous Judge and my Advocate at the throne of God. I trust Him with my time, talents, and treasures. He always judges rightly.

⚔ All that has been taken is being redeemed and restored (Joel 2:25). Restitution is mine as the Lord repays with interest those who love Him and are called by His name (Proverbs 6:31).

20

BATTLE CRY FOR FAVOR

May the favor of the Lord our God rest on us;
establish the work of our hands for us—yes, establish
the work of our hands (Psalm 90:17 NIV).

By grace I have been saved and not of my own efforts or accomplishments, but Yours, Jesus (Ephesians 2:8-9). I know that grace is unmerited favor. I don't deserve it but I gladly accept it as a gift from You, Lord. In Your extravagance, You have promised me fullness and favor upon favor (John 1:16) because You love to multiply Your blessings. You will never pass me by or forget my need (Genesis 18:3). I know You will answer my requests because You know me by name (Exodus 33:17).

Through Your hand of grace on me, I will stand in the presence of kings (1 Samuel 16:22) and testify to Your power. As I follow Your will and Your way for me, I am increasing in wisdom and stature, and in favor with God and men (Luke 2:52) just as You did, Lord Jesus, as You walked out Your assignment on earth. My fervent prayer is to be in alignment for my Kingdom assignment so that I can bring You a full reward when I stand at Your throne. Do not let one soul be lost that You have assigned to me. Because You keep Your promises, You are prospering me and blessing my generations (Genesis 26:3) to bless others.

I pray that You show me mercy. Bless me with the favor to do all things with excellence especially in dark and desperate places (Psalm 103:22). Though it looks like I am in bondage, Jesus, You are working all things for my good (Romans 8:28). Freedom and upgrade into higher authority and assignments are my reward as I serve You with gladness and my earthly masters with humility (Genesis 39:4). You are holding out the golden scepter of Your presence to me (Esther 5:2). I can boldly come into the throne room—the Holy of Holies—because of Your grace on my life. I am blessed indeed. Thank You, Lord, and amen.

SCRIPTURES

Psalm 5:12 (NKJV) – *For You, O Lord, will bless the righteous; with favor You will surround him as with a shield.*

Psalm 84:11 (NIV) – *For the Lord God is a sun and shield; the Lord bestows favor and honor; no good thing does he withhold from those whose walk is blameless.*

Psalm 30:5 (NKJV) – *For His anger is but for a moment, His favor is for life; weeping may endure for a night, but joy comes in the morning.*

Ephesians 1:11 (NKJV) – *In Him also we have obtained an inheritance* **[favor],** *being predestined according to the purpose of Him who works all things according to the counsel of His will.*

Genesis 19:19 (NKJV) – *Indeed now, your servant has found favor in your sight, and you have increased your* *mercy which you have shown me by saving my life; but I cannot escape to the mountains, lest some evil overtake me and I die.*

Isaiah 49:8 (NIV) – *This is what the Lord says: "In the time of my favor I will answer you, and in the day of salvation I will help you; I will keep you and will make you to be a covenant for the people to restore the land and to reassign its desolate inheritances."*

Isaiah 58:11 (NKJV) – *The Lord will guide you continually, and satisfy your soul in drought, and strengthen your bones; you shall be like a watered garden, and like a spring of water, whose waters do not fail.*

Joshua 1:8 (NKJV) – *This Book of the Law shall not depart from your mouth, but you shall meditate in it day and night, that you may observe to do according to all that is written in it. For then you will make your way prosperous, and then you will have good success.*

Proverbs 16:15 (NKJV) – *In the light of the king's face is life, and his favor is like a cloud of the latter rain.*

I DECLARE IN THE MIGHTY NAME OF KING JESUS:

- You have given me a purpose and a promise. I am growing in stature, goodwill, and favor with the Lord and with people (1 Samuel 2:26; Daniel 1:9).

- Because I value wisdom, the favor of God is upon me (Proverbs 8:35).

- Humility is the currency of Heaven. The way to the throne room is though the servant's quarters (Proverbs 3:34).

- Jesus has delivered me out of my troubles. With the Lord's favor and wisdom, I am being positioned for my Kingdom purpose and destiny (Acts 7:10).

- I do not fear my future. I have found favor with God (Luke 1:30).

- The Lord is giving me victory over my enemies. The spoils of war are mine and I will not leave the battlefield empty-handed (Exodus 3:21).

- The Lord is my everlasting light and my God is my glory. I can see in the supernatural what others cannot in the natural because He illuminates my way (Isaiah 60:19).

- I am a person of excellence. I will stand before kings and not unknown men (Proverbs 22:29).

- The Lord has made me to be a well springing up. I will bless and refresh those around me with the everlasting water of the Holy Spirit (Numbers 21:17).

- Whatever I set my hand to prospers because the God of Eternity is mine (Ecclesiastes 9:10).

- My good works will glorify only Him.

- The Lord is blessing me indeed. He is increasing my territory with His hand of favor and keeping me from evil so that I would not cause others pain (1 Chronicles 4:10).

21

BATTLE CRY FOR A FATHER'S HEART

And he will turn the hearts of the fathers to the children,
and the hearts of the children to their fathers, lest I come
and strike the earth with a curse (Malachi 4:6 NKJV).

Abba, You are good. You have called me to be "a chosen generation, a royal priesthood" to proclaim your praises and call my family out of darkness into Your marvelous light (1 Peter 2:9). I thank You for being a strong tower from the enemy. I will trust in the shelter of Your wings (Psalm 61:3-4). Lord, I want to be a tower of strength and shelter in the storm for my children. Just as You carried me through the wilderness, teach me to carry my family out of dangerous places and into Your presence (Deuteronomy 1:31).

You are my Father (2 Corinthians 6:18). I will not be conformed to this world, but be transformed by the renewing of my mind. For my family's sake, I want to do Your good, acceptable, and perfect will (Romans 12:2). I will be sober and vigilant in protecting their hearts and minds from those who steal, kill, and destroy (1 Peter 5:8). As you have compassion on Your children, I will have compassion on mine (Psalm 103:13). We will love what You love and hate what You hate. You have taught me the way of wisdom and led me in right paths. Help me to do the same with the children You have entrusted to me so they will not stumble (Proverbs 4:11-12).

Help me to instruct my family—to guide them with Your Word and Holy Spirit (Psalm 32:7-8). I will be strong and courageous because I know You are with me as I lead my children (Joshua 1:9) and honor their mother. I will not let them forsake her love and laws (Proverbs 1:8). I receive my children and the assignment You have given me as a father so I can receive You, Jesus (Luke 9:47-48). You are the Way, the Truth, and the Life. We will walk in Your blessings for a thousand generations (Exodus 20:6), and I will speak life into them as You have spoken life into me.

SCRIPTURES

1 Corinthians 13:11 (NKJV) – *When I was a child, I spoke as a child, I understood as a child, I thought as a child; but when I became a man, I put away childish things.*

1 Timothy 6:11 (NKJV) – *But you, O man of God, flee these things and pursue righteousness, godliness, faith, love, patience, gentleness.*

Matthew 7:9-10 (NKJV) – *Or what man is there among you who, if his son asks for bread, will give him a stone? Or if he asks for a fish, will he give him a serpent?*

1 Corinthians 11:1 (NKJV) – *Imitate me, just as I also imitate Christ.*

Ephesians 6:4 (NKJV) – *And you, fathers, do not provoke your children to wrath, but bring them up in the training and admonition of the Lord.*

Genesis 18:19 (NKJV) – *For I have known him, in order that he may command his children and his household after him, that they keep the way of the Lord, to do righteousness and justice, that the Lord may bring to Abraham what He has spoken to him.*

Deuteronomy 6:6-7 (NKJV) – *And these words which I command you today shall be in your heart. You shall teach them diligently to your children, and shall talk of them when you sit in your house, when you walk by the way, when you lie down, and when you rise up.*

Proverbs 22:6 (NKJV) – *Train up a child in the way he should go, and when he is old he will not depart from it.*

Psalm 119:9 (NKJV) – *How can a young man cleanse his way? By taking heed according to Your word.*

Luke 15:20 (NKJV) – *And he arose and came to his father. But when he was still a great way off, his father saw him and had compassion, and ran and fell on his neck and kissed him.*

Hebrews 12:7 (NKJV) – *If you endure chastening, God deals with you as with sons; for what son is there whom a father does not chasten?*

I DECLARE IN THE MIGHTY NAME OF KING JESUS:

✝ I am a godly leader of my family. If you've seen me, you've seen the Father.

✝ I am a gardener and my family is my "guarded space." I will rip out every lie of the enemy and plant the truth of Jesus. Where there is fear, I will plant faith. Where there is self-doubt, I will plant confidence. Where there is confusion, I will plant identity. Where there is hopelessness, I will plant destiny. I will speak life and not death; blessings not curses.

✝ I have a spirit of power, love, and a sound mind. I walk in the wisdom and favor of the Father. My generations will follow in His footsteps.

✝ I declare a Psalm 91 hedge of protection over myself and my family. Jesus is our Deliverer and Salvation.

✝ My family will understand and walk in the power and authority given them by King Jesus. We are sons, daughters, and joint heirs with Jesus.

✝ My generations will be protected from temptation. We will not be overtaken by addiction or worldly thinking.

✝ My sons will honor, respect, and love the women in their lives; and my daughters will know they are special and loved.

✝ Neither failure nor success define our worth. My generations are loved and accepted even when they fall. I will pick them up as You have lifted me up, Abba.

🗡 My bloodline will have a heart to know the Father. We will fulfill our purpose and bring King Jesus a 100-fold harvest.

22

BATTLE CRY FOR SALVATION

For God so loved the world that He gave His only begotten
Son, that whoever believes in Him should not perish
but have everlasting life. For God did not send His Son
into the world to condemn the world, but that the world
through Him might be saved (John 3:16-17 NKJV).

Father, I thank You for the priceless gift of salvation and for sending Your Son, Jesus, to die for our sins. It is Your wish for none to be lost, so I ask You to give _____ revelation knowledge of You. Pull down every stronghold of the enemy that keeps them from receiving Your saving grace and cause every high thing coming between their heart and the Gospel to be melted away by Your Holy Spirit fire.

I come against the powers of darkness blinding _____ from receiving Your salvation, Jesus, and command you, prince of the power of the air, to be gone in the name of King Jesus. Prince of Peace, I ask You to invade their atmosphere and silence the lies of the enemy. Give _____ dreams and supernatural encounters with You. Lord, open their eyes to their own spiritual condition and activate the piece of eternity You have placed in their heart. Just as deep calls unto deep, Jesus, I pray the everlasting in You calls out to the everlasting in them, awakening them to Your real life and transformation.

Father, bring _____ from the kingdom of darkness into the Kingdom of light and cause Your plan and purpose for their life to be made manifest. Convict them so they will see the Truth. Correct them and train them in righteousness so they can walk out every step of the destiny You planned for them long ago. Holy Spirit, surround _____ with those who love You and will testify to Your mercy in every season. Send righteous people who have experienced Your goodness to provoke them to jealousy. Jesus, I ask You to overwhelm them with Your mercy and grace so that they would repent and be saved. Thank You, Lord, for answering my prayers in Jesus's name. Amen.

SCRIPTURES

John 3:3 (NKJV) – *Jesus answered and said to him, "Most assuredly, I say to you, unless one is born again, he cannot see the kingdom of God."*

John 5:24 (NKJV) – *Most assuredly, I say to you, he who hears My word and believes in Him who sent Me has everlasting life, and shall not come into judgment, but has passed from death into life.*

John 14:6 (NKJV) – *Jesus said to him, "I Am the way, the truth, and the life. No one comes to the Father except through Me."*

Acts 4:12 (NKJV) – *Nor is there salvation in any other, for there is no other name* **[Jesus]** *under heaven given among men by which we must be saved.*

Acts 16:31 (NKJV) – *So they said, "Believe on the Lord Jesus Christ, and you will be saved, you and your household."*

Romans 5:8 (NKJV) – *But God demonstrates His own love toward us, in that while we were still sinners, Christ died for us.*

Romans 6:23 (NKJV) – *For the wages of sin is death, but the gift of God is eternal life in Christ Jesus our Lord.*

Romans 10:9 (NKJV) – *If you confess with your mouth the Lord Jesus and believe in your heart that God has raised Him from the dead, you will be saved.*

Ephesians 1:13 (NKJV) – *In Him you also trusted, after you heard the word of truth, the gospel of your salvation; in whom also, having believed, you were sealed with the Holy Spirit of promise.*

Ephesians 2:8-9 (NKJV) – *For by grace you have been saved through faith, and that not of yourselves; it is the gift of God, not of works, lest anyone should boast.*

2 Timothy 1:9 (NKJV) – *Who has saved us and called us with a holy calling, not according to our works, but according to His own purpose and grace which given to us in Christ Jesus before time began.*

I DECLARE IN THE MIGHTY NAME OF KING JESUS:

✝ Now is the day of salvation for _____ (2 Corinthians 6:2). They will come to repentance and will not perish (2 Peter 3:9).

✝ I decree the conviction and correction of the Holy Spirit over _____'s life, that they would be redeemed and trained in righteousness (2 Timothy 3:16).

✝ I declare all curses, vows and iniquities keeping _____ from a saving knowledge of Jesus broken in Jesus's name.

✝ I proclaim all misconceptions and mental myths clouding their thoughts are cast down. They are being replaced with a sound mind free of enemy interference.

✝ I declare _____ is a child of the Most High God (John 1:12). You created them before the earth was formed and gave them an identity, purpose, and destiny. I call these things forth in Jesus's mighty name.

✝ I decree all guilt, shame, and fear be rooted out of _____'s heart and mind. A Spirit of power, love, and a sound mind are theirs (2 Timothy 1:7).

✝ I proclaim darkness and deceit would hold no joy for _____. Cause them to crave life over death and sunshine over shadows.

✝ _____ was not made for Your wrath (John 3:36). They will be clothed in white garments and You will never blot their name out of the Lamb's Book of Life (Revelation 3:5).

† You are the Author and the Finisher of _____'s faith (Hebrews 12:2). They are a "living epistle" and their life will testify to Your saving grace (2 Corinthians 3:2).

† The salvation of the righteous is from You, Lord. You are _____' s stronghold in times of trouble (Psalm 37:39). They will call on Your name and You will never cast them out (John 6:37; Romans 10:13).

23

BATTLE CRY FOR GOVERNMENT AND ISRAEL

Therefore I exhort first of all that supplications, prayers, intercessions, and giving of thanks be made for all men, for kings and all who are in authority, that we may lead a quiet and peaceable life in all godliness and reverence (1 Timothy 2:1-2 NKJV).

Lord, I come before You praying for the president, vice president, and all in his cabinet. I pray for our governors, mayors, court justices, and military leaders. I ask, Lord, that You bless them with Your wisdom, lead them by Your Holy Spirit, giving them Your strength and Your desire to help those who have no advocates. Direct them to do what is right and just in Your eyes that this land might be blessed with sound leadership.

I ask You to remove dishonest officials striving to fulfill their own desires instead of the good of the people they serve. Reveal their secrets and expose their wickedness so they might be convicted and corrected, or removed from office.

Help me to observe the laws willingly and cheerfully, upholding, respecting, and appreciating the leaders and law enforcement agencies who carry out these laws—that I may lead a tranquil, peaceful life. In Jesus's name.

SCRIPTURES

Psalm 75:7 (NKJV) – *God is the Judge: He puts down one, and exalts another.*

Proverbs 8:15-16 (NKJV) –*By me kings reign, and rulers decree justice. By me princes rule, and nobles, all the judges of the earth.*

Mark 12:17 (NKJV) – *And Jesus answered and said to them, "Render to Caesar the things that are Caesar's, and to God the things that are God's." And they marveled at Him.*

Titus 3:1-2 (NKJV) – *Remind them to be subject to rulers and authorities, to obey, to be ready for every good work, to speak evil of no one, to be peaceable, gentle, showing all humility to all men.*

Proverbs 29:25-26 (NKJV) – *The fear of man brings a snare, but whoever trusts in the Lord shall be safe. Many seek the ruler's favor, but justice for man comes from the Lord.*

Psalm 9:7-10 (NIV) – *The Lord reigns forever; he has established his throne for judgment. He rules the world in righteousness and judges the peoples with equity. The Lord is a refuge for the oppressed, a stronghold in times of trouble. Those who know your name trust in you, for you, Lord, have never forsaken those who seek you.*

Matthew 20:25-28 (NKJV) – *But Jesus called them to Himself and said, "You know that the rulers of the Gentiles lord it over them, and those who are great exercise authority over them. Yet it shall not be so among you;*

but whoever desires to become great among you, let him be your servant. And whoever desires to be first among you, let him be your slave—just as the Son of Man did not come to be served, but to serve, and to give His life a ransom for many."

1 Peter 2:15-17 (NKJV) – *For this is the will of God, that by doing good you may put to silence the ignorance of foolish men—as free, yet not using liberty as a cloak for vice, but as bondservants of God. Honor all people. Love the brotherhood. Fear God. Honor the king.*

I DECLARE IN THE MIGHTY NAME OF KING JESUS:

✝ There is no authority apart from You. You are in control.

✝ Your justice, truth, and integrity on our leaders—that they may be godly men and women seeking to serve You first.

✝ Sound judgment and godly wisdom throughout our justice system and halls of government at every level.

✝ I will give to the government what is due it and I will give to You what is Yours, Father God.

✝ I submit to those in authority so I can live a peaceable life. I trust in You, Lord, because justice comes from You alone!

✝ I will do good and put to silence the ignorance of foolish people.

- I will honor all people. I will love my brothers and sisters in Christ, I will fear You, God, and honor those in governmental authority.

- I will honor and support Your chosen nation, Israel. I will pray for her leaders, her people, and her awakening to you as the one true Messiah.

- I stand with my natural brothers and sisters, the Jewish people—"the sands of the seashore"—as your supernatural child—"the stars of the sky." I will bless them and honor them, openly declaring Your love for them and the nation of Israel.

24

BATTLE CRY FOR FAMILY HERITAGE AND LEGACY

Honor your father and your mother, so that you may live long in the land the Lord your God is giving you (Exodus 20:12 NIV).

Father God, I thank You for the parents You gave to me. I call them blessed in Jesus's name. I thank You for giving me a love and respect for my parents that only You can give. I thank You for showing me how to give my children a godly heritage to love You with all of their heart, soul, mind, and strength (Deuteronomy 6:5). I praise You that I can pass it to the next generation by walking a life of righteousness and integrity. Lord, I have no greater joy than to see my children walking in truth. Thank You that children are a heritage from You.

Thank You that, as Your child, I have the heritage of knowing the enemy cannot form any weapon against me and my family. You will condemn every tongue that rises up against us (Isaiah 54:17)! Help me, Lord, to never forget Your teachings. Seeking and meditating on them will assure me a long life ending in peace (Proverbs 3:1-2). In Jesus's name. Amen.

SCRIPTURES

Proverbs 23:22 (NKJV) – *Listen to your father who begot you, and do not despise your mother when she is old.*

Psalm 37:18 (ESV) – *The Lord knows the days of the blameless, and their heritage will remain forever.*

Proverbs 20:7 (NKJV) – *The righteous man walks in his integrity; his children are blessed after him.*

Genesis 2:24 (NKJV) – *Therefore a man shall leave his father and mother and be joined to his wife, and they shall become one flesh.*

Psalm 127:3-5 (NKJV) – *Behold, children are a heritage from the Lord, the fruit of the womb is a reward. Like arrows in the hand of a warrior, so are the children of one's youth. Happy is the man who has his quiver is full of them....*

Proverbs 23:25 (NKJV) – *Let your father and your mother be glad, and let her who bore you rejoice.*

Ephesians 6:4 (NKJV) – *And you, fathers, do not provoke your children to wrath, but bring them up in the training and admonition of the Lord.*

Proverbs 17:6 (NKJV) – *Children's children are the crown of old men, and the glory of children is their father.*

Titus 2:1-8 (NKJV) – *But as for you, speak the things which are proper for sound doctrine: that the older men be sober, reverent, temperate, sound in faith, in love, in patience; the older women likewise, that they be reverent in behavior, not slanderers, not given to much wine,* *teachers of good things—that they admonish the young women to love their husbands, to love their children, to be discreet, chaste, homemakers, good, obedient to their own husbands, that the word of God may not be blasphemed. Likewise, exhort the young men to be sober-minded, in all things showing yourself to be a pattern of good works; in doctrine showing integrity, reverence, incorruptibility, sound speech that cannot be condemned, that one who is an opponent may be ashamed, having nothing evil to say of you.*

I DECLARE IN THE MIGHTY NAME OF KING JESUS:

✝ Wisdom to lead by example, Lord, with a servant's heart just like Yours.

✝ I will honor my parents that I may live long.

✝ I will honor the widows in my family as this pleases You, Lord.

✝ I will love You, Lord, and teach those in my household to follow You with a full heart.

✝ I will love and respect my spouse, serving and praying for my beloved's daily needs.

✝ I will walk in unity with my spouse, becoming one together.

✝ I will bless my parents, my children and spouse— not curse them. I will speak life, not death, over my household.

⚔ I will not exasperate my children, leaving them without hope. I will encourage them to use their gifts and talents for Your purpose.

⚔ I will show mercy, forgiveness, and restoration to my family as You have done to me.

⚔ I will love You, God, with all of my heart, soul, mind, and strength, and be the leader You have made me to be.

⚔ As for me and my house, we shall serve the Lord.

25

Battle Cry for Justice and Protection

This poor man called, and the Lord heard him, and saved him out of all his troubles (Psalm 34:6 NIV).

You are Jehovah Sabaoth, the Lord of Hosts. You are my Protector and You will battle for me (1 Samuel 30:23). I pray a Psalm 91 supernatural hedge of protection around myself, my family, and my circumstances. The battle belongs to You, Lord (1 Samuel 17:47).

You are also Jehovah Tsidkenu, the Righteous One. You oversee the house of the wicked and cast them down to ruin (Proverbs 21:12). As the Righteous Judge (Psalm 7:11), You alone can bring justice to me. I pray a Psalm 7 prayer of justice over myself and my circumstances that You will rise in Your anger, O Lord, and stand against the fury of my enemies to deliver me.

SCRIPTURES

Psalm 33:5 (NIV) – *The Lord loves righteousness and justice; the earth is full of his unfailing love.*

Job 34:12 (NKJV) – *Surely God will never do wickedly, nor will the Almighty pervert justice.*

Psalm 7:6 (NLT) – *Arise, O Lord, in anger! Stand up against the fury of my enemies! Wake up, my God, and bring justice!*

Isaiah 11:4 (NKJV) – *But with righteousness He shall judge the poor, and decide with equity for the meek of the earth; He shall strike the earth with the rod of His mouth, and with the breath of His lips He shall slay the wicked.*

Isaiah 16:5 (ESV) – *Then a throne will be established in steadfast love, and on it will sit in faithfulness in the tent of David one who judges and seeks justice and is swift to do righteousness.*

Deuteronomy 30:3 (NKJV) – *Then the Lord your God will bring you back from captivity, and have compassion on you, and gather you again from all the nations where the Lord your God has scattered you.*

I DECLARE IN THE MIGHTY NAME OF KING JESUS:

- No weapon fashioned against me shall prosper (Isaiah 54:17).

- You are my strong tower. I run into You and am saved (Proverbs 18:10).

✝ All fear, anxiety, and unbelief have been displaced by faith, confidence, and thankfulness in my heart (Philippians 4:6-7).

✝ That You would give back the days the locusts have eaten (Joel 2:25) and restore what the enemy has stolen from me (Deuteronomy 30:3).

✝ Justice will roll like a river and righteousness like a never-failing stream on my behalf (Amos 5:24).

✝ I will see the goodness of God in the land of the living (Psalm 27:13) and victorious angelic warfare over me. Sir, I release Your angels to do Your will in my life (2 Corinthians 10:3).

✝ I will walk in a Joshua anointing. I will have great victory in the days, months, and years to come (Numbers 27:18).

✝ My intimacy with You will produce long-awaited results and breakthrough in my life (Hosea 6:6; Jeremiah 9:24).

✝ Supernatural sanity over my mind, heart, and emotions because I have the mind of Christ (1 Corinthians 2:16).

✝ I declare a Psalm 91 hedge of protection around my body, mind and spirit:

Whoever dwells in the shelter of the Most High will rest in the shadow of the Almighty. I will say of the Lord, "He is my refuge and my fortress, my God, in whom I trust." Surely he will save you from the fowler's snare and from the deadly pestilence. He will cover you with his feathers, and under his wings you will find refuge; his faithfulness will be your shield and rampart. You will not fear the terror of night, nor the arrow that flies by day, nor the pestilence that stalks in the darkness, nor the plague that destroys at midday. A thousand may fall at your side, ten thousand at your right hand, but it will not come near you. You will only observe with your eyes and see the punishment of the wicked. If you say, "The Lord is my refuge," and you make the Most High your dwelling, no harm will overtake you, no disaster will come near your tent. For he will command his angels concerning you to guard you in all your ways; they will lift you up in their hands, so that you will not strike your foot against a stone. You will tread on the lion and the cobra; you will trample the great lion and the serpent. "Because he loves me," says the Lord, "I will rescue him; I will protect him, for he acknowledges my name. He will call on me, and I will answer him; I will be with him in trouble, I will deliver him and honor him. With long life I will satisfy him and show him my salvation" **(Psalm 91:1-16 NIV).**

26

BATTLE CRY FOR RESCUE AND DELIVERANCE

Because he has set his love upon Me, therefore I will deliver him; I will set him on high, because he has known My name. He shall call upon Me, and I will answer him; I will be with him in trouble; I will deliver him and honor him. With long life I will satisfy him, and show him My salvation (Psalm 91:14-16 NKJV).

Lord, I thank You that You are my salvation. You are the only One who can deliver me from my circumstances. You are my Rock and my Strong Tower. You are worthy of all my praise! Thank You for Your Psalm 91 hedge of protection around me and my family. Lord, as I cry out to You, I know You hear me and are delivering me out of all of my troubles (Psalm 34:17).

Lord, I thank You that, as a child of God, You have given me authority to cast out demons, heal the sick, raise the dead, and cleanse the lepers. Freely, You have given and freely I receive (Matthew 10:8).

Where You have made me free I am free indeed! I look for the new thing that is coming, for rivers in the desert and highways in the wilderness (Isaiah 43:19). Lord, You are the Rock that is higher than I (Psalm 61:2). I look to you and I throw myself upon the Rock of my salvation. Break me so I can be used to bring many to You, for Your glory. In Jesus's name. Amen.

SCRIPTURES

Psalm 18:2 (NKJV) – *The Lord is my rock and my fortress and my deliverer; my God, my strength, in whom I will trust; my shield and the horn of my salvation, my stronghold.*

Deuteronomy 20:4 (NKJV) – *For the Lord your God is He who goes with you, to fight for you against your enemies, to save you.*

Psalm 50:15 (NKJV) – *Call upon Me in the day of trouble; I will deliver you, and you shall glorify Me.*

Colossians 1:13 (NKJV) – *He has delivered us from the power of darkness and conveyed us into the kingdom of the Son of His love.*

2 Thessalonians 3:3 (NKJV) – *But the Lord is faithful, who will establish you and guard you from the evil one.*

Luke 10:19 (NKJV) – *Behold, I give you the authority to trample on serpents and scorpions, and over all the power of the enemy, and nothing shall by any means hurt you.*

Isaiah 41:10 (NKJV) – *Fear not, for I am with you; be not dismayed, for I am your God. I will strengthen you, Yes, I will help you, I will uphold you with My righteous right hand.*

Psalm 40:2 (NKJV) – *He also brought me up out of a horrible pit, out of the miry clay, and set my feet upon a rock, and established my steps.*

Psalm 40:17 (NKJV) – *But I am poor and needy; yet the Lord thinks upon me. You are my help and my deliverer; do not delay, O my God.*

Psalm 143:9 (NKJV) – *Deliver me, O Lord, from my enemies; in You I take shelter.*

2 Samuel 22:2-4 (NKJV) – *And he said: "The Lord is my rock and my fortress and my deliverer; the God of my strength, in whom I will trust; my shield and the horn of my salvation, my stronghold and my refuge; my Savior, You save me from violence. I will call upon the Lord, who is worthy to be praised; so shall I be saved from my enemies."*

I DECLARE IN THE MIGHTY NAME OF KING JESUS:

† As I call upon Your name, You hear me and deliver me (Psalm 34:17). I shall know the Truth and the Truth shall set me free! (John 8:32).

† Because You hear me, I will be delivered from all my fears! (Psalm 34:4).

† You, Lord, will not delay in delivering me! (2 Peter 3:9). Because the Son set me free, I am free indeed! (John 8:36).

† You are my Strong Tower. I run to You and am saved (Psalm 18:10). No weapon fashioned against me shall prosper (Isaiah 54:17).

- I will have dominion in the days, weeks, and years to come.

- I will advance to new heights and obstacles will be removed in Your name (Psalm 46:2).

- I am not afraid because You are with me. Your rod keeps my enemies at bay. Your staff keeps me near. You anoint my head with the oil of health. You call me family. My cup runs over because You are my Shepherd (Psalm 23).

27

BATTLE CRY FOR THE NEXT GENERATION

Train up a child in the way he should go, and when he is old he will not depart from it (Proverbs 22:6 NKJV).

I praise You, God Almighty! I thank You for the next generation being raised up in the admonition of the Lord (Ephesians 6:4). I thank You for children who honor their father and their mother, that it will go well with them and they may live long on the earth (Ephesians 6:2-3). I thank You for children who are wise, love others, walk in humility, and obey their parents. I thank You for children who are thankful, who walk in holiness and love You, Lord.

Lord, where my children are walking in rebellion, draw them back to You as the prodigal children they are. Reveal Yourself to them in a new way and reveal Your truth to them, that they will return to walk in the destiny and purpose You created them for before the foundations of the world. I ask that they would glorify You! In Jesus's name!

SCRIPTURES

Deuteronomy 6:5-7 (NKJV) – *You shall love the Lord your God with all your heart, with all your soul, and with all your strength. And these words which I command you today shall be in your heart. You shall teach them diligently to your children, and shall talk of them when you sit in your house, when you walk by the way, when you lie down, and when you rise up.*

Ephesians 6:1-3 (NKJV) – *Children, obey your parents in the Lord, for this is right. "Honor your father and mother," which is the first commandment with promise: "that it may be well with you and you may live long on the earth."*

Proverbs 23:24 (NKJV) – *The father of the righteous will greatly rejoice, and he who begets a wise child will delight in him.*

Ephesians 6:4 (NKJV) – *And you, fathers, do not provoke your children to wrath, but bring them up in the training and admonition of the Lord.*

Joshua 24:15 (NKJV) – *...As for me and my house, we will serve the Lord.*

Proverbs 29:17 (NIV) – *Discipline your children, and they will give you peace; they will bring you the delights you desire.*

Isaiah 38:19 (NIV) – *The living, the living—they praise you, as I am doing today; parents tell their children about your faithfulness.*

Proverbs 29:15 (NKJV) – *The rod and rebuke give wisdom, but a child left to himself brings shame to his mother.*

Proverbs 1:8-9 (NIV) – *Listen, my son, to your father's instruction and do not forsake your mother's teaching. They are a garland to grace your head and a chain to adorn your neck.*

I DECLARE IN THE MIGHTY NAME OF KING JESUS:

† That I delight in my children! They are a joy and gift from You, Lord. My children walk in obedience to those in authority.

† My children walk in wisdom and humility. They have the mind of Christ!

† My children walk in love—mine and that of their heavenly Father. My children know the Truth and the Truth has set them free!

† My children walk in the salvation of the Lord, testifying of Your goodness!

† My children will see visions and prophesy unto the Lord, bringing comfort and edification to those in need.

† My children will seek wise counsel, love Your Word, and follow You with a full heart for all of their days.

✝ I will recognize and nurture the gifts and calling You, Lord, have given my children. They will fulfill their destiny in You!

✝ I will not exasperate my children leaving them without hope. Instead, I will lift them up with words of encouragement and affirmation.

✝ I will speak only life over my children. I will not curse them. As for me and my house, we will serve the Lord!

28

Battle Cry for the Body of Christ

*And He put all things under His feet, and gave Him to be head
over all things to the church, which is His body, the fullness
of Him who fills all in all* (Ephesians 1:22-23 NKJV).

I come before You, Jesus, our High Priest and King (Hebrews 7:13-17), asking for unity for the Church. Your final wish on earth was for the church to be one, as the Trinity is One (John 17:22). Unify Your message through us and let Your Holy Spirit descend on the Church, so that untold thousands would see our love for each other and for the nations (John 13:35). Let the Church be a river in the desert and a highway in the wilderness, so that none would be thirsty or lost (Isaiah 43:19).

The Church is not a cruise ship. It was made for battle. Let us rise up in these dark days and fight for the souls of the lost. Let us drag prisoners of Your enemy from the flames of slavery and death, into the light and love of your family. As we have many members (1 Corinthians 12:14), Jesus bring us together in purpose, working fearlessly and flawlessly to bring You honor, glory, and the promise of souls who need salvation.

Jesus, You are the Bridegroom. We, the Church, are Your bride (Revelation 19:7). By Your sacrifice, we have been made holy. Help us to prepare for Your return. Let our lamps never run out of oil, that we would be joyous participants in the coming marriage supper of the Lamb (Matthew 25:1-13). You are our Head (Ephesians 5:23). Let us serve You with joy, always seeking to increase Your Kingdom and bring Heaven to earth.

SCRIPTURES

1 Corinthians 12:12-13 (ESV) – *For just as the body is one and has many members, and all the members of the body, though many, are one body, so it is with Christ. For in one Spirit we were all baptized into one body—Jews or Greeks, slaves or free—and all were made to drink of one Spirit.*

Romans 15:5-6 (NKJV) – *Now may the God of patience and comfort grant you to be like-minded toward one another, according to Christ Jesus, that you may with one mind and one mouth glorify the God and Father of our Lord Jesus Christ.*

Luke 10:19 (ESV) – *Behold, I have given you authority to tread on serpents and scorpions, and over all the power of the enemy, and nothing shall hurt you.*

Isaiah 54:17 (NKJV) – *"No weapon formed against you shall prosper, and every tongue which rises against you in judgment you shall condemn. This is the heritage of the servants of the Lord, And their righteousness is from Me," says the Lord.*

Ephesians 4:1-6 (NKJV) – *I, therefore, the prisoner of the Lord, beseech you to walk worthy of the calling with which you were called, with all lowliness and gentleness,* *with long suffering, bearing with one another in love, endeavoring to keep the unity of the Spirit in the bond of peace. There is one body and one Spirit, just as you were called in one hope of your calling; one Lord, one faith, one baptism; one God and Father of all, who is above all, and through all, and in you all.*

I DECLARE IN THE MIGHTY NAME OF KING JESUS:

✝ Unity over the Church, that we would work together to defeat the enemy by bringing Good News to the lost and hurting.

✝ Revival is here. I am a willing member of the body of Christ. I was made for such a time as this.

✝ My vision is clear. My assignment is certain. I will be a witness of Your goodness to the nations.

✝ I am fully prepared for the battle at hand. I wear the full armor of God. Increase my territory!

✝ I am not afraid. No weapon formed against me, or the Church, shall prosper.

✝ The gates of hell will not overwhelm me. The enemy is defeated.

✝ The gift of prophecy is mine. I will speak Your words to strengthen, encourage, and comfort people's souls and bring them to repentance.

✝ All wisdom, knowledge, and discernment are my inheritance from You.

✝ I am Your beloved and You are mine! I await the arrival of my Groom and my destiny.

✝ I am prepared for the coming King. My lamp will never run dry!

✝ The Holy Spirit in me is rising up. I will partner with Him to bring a harvest in these great days of revival.

29

BATTLE CRY FOR VICTORY OVER PRIDE AND SELFISHNESS

Let no one seek his own, but each one the other's
well-being (1 Corinthians 10:24 NKJV).

Father God, in a day when it seems "everyone looks out for their own interests, not those of Jesus Christ" (Philippians 2:21 NIV), I seek Your hand and Your heart for myself and others. Cause me to fulfill Your law by bearing the burdens of those in my circle of influence (Galatians 6:2). Help me to crucify my flesh with its worldly passions and selfish desires so I will truly belong to You (Galatians 5:24).

Give me the strength to obey righteousness and truth, and put away self-seeking out of fear or ambition (Romans 2:8). Jesus, today I deny my selfish pride and take up the cross of humility to follow You (Luke 9:23). Humility is the currency of Heaven and I want my account to be full. I will not forget to do good and to share, for with such sacrifices God is well pleased (Hebrews 13:16).

Like You, I will support the weak by remembering "it is more blessed to give than to receive" (Acts 20:35). I will not compare myself to others, which only leads to condemnation (2 Corinthians 10:12). I refuse to covet in my heart (Psalm 119:36). Holy Spirit, convict and correct me when I boast in the flesh for people's attention and affection (Galatians 6:12-13), for my flesh lusts against the Spirit, and the Spirit against my flesh (Galatians 5:17). I repent of boasting, pride, and self-seeking so others will see Christ Jesus in me and be saved. Amen.

SCRIPTURES

John 15:13 (NKJV) – *Greater love has no one than this, than to lay down one's life for his friends.*

James 3:16 (NKJV) – *For where envy and self-seeking exist, confusion and every evil thing are there.*

Mark 12:31 (NKJV) – *And the second, like it, is this: "You shall love your neighbor as yourself." There is no other commandment greater than these.*

Proverbs 11:25 (NKJV) – *The generous soul will be made rich, and he who waters will also be watered himself.*

Proverbs 18:1 (NKJV) – *A man who isolates himself seeks his own desire; he rages against all wise judgment.*

Philippians 2:3-4 (NKJV) – *Let nothing be done through selfish ambition or conceit, but in lowliness of mind let each esteem others better than himself. Let each of you look out not only for his own interests, but also for the interests of others.*

Proverbs 16:18 (NKJV) – *Pride goes before destruction, and a haughty spirit before a fall.*

James 4:6 (NKJV) – *...God resists the proud, but gives grace to the humble.*

Jeremiah 9:23-24 (NKJV) – *Thus says the Lord: "Let not the wise man glory in his wisdom, let not the mighty man glory in his might, nor let the rich man glory in his riches; but let him who glories glory in this, that he understands and knows Me, that I am the Lord, exercising lovingkindness, judgment, and righteousness in the earth. For in these I delight," says the Lord.*

I DECLARE IN THE MIGHTY NAME OF KING JESUS:

- † I do not walk in lusts of the world or the pride of life. I am not of this world, but of the Father (1 John 2:16).

- † The love of God is within me. I open my heart and hand to those in need (1 John 3:17).

- † I bring justice to the poor, oppressed, widow and orphan. I love mercy and seek to walk humbly with my God (Micah 6:8).

- † I live according to the Spirit. I speak life and peace because my mind is set on God's law and things above. I please the Lord, not humans (Romans 8:5-9).

- † I testify to the Gospel of God's grace. I do not hold this life dear, but run my race for the joy of Jesus, which is set before me (Acts 20:24).

✝ I sow to the Spirit so I will reap everlasting life. I refuse to sow in my flesh and will not reap corruption (Galatians 6:8).

✝ I am wise because I embrace humility. I will not be shamed by walking in pride (Proverbs 11:2).

✝ I am strong because I bear the burdens of the weak. I do not please myself. I comfort and edify my neighbors for their good and Christ's glory (Romans 15:1-3).

✝ The opposite of love is not hate; it is selfishness. I renounce my selfish ways and commit to the way of love (1 Corinthians 13:4-6) by loving God and others (Luke 10:27).

30

BATTLE CRY FOR THE SPIRIT OF THE LORD

The Spirit of the Lord shall rest upon Him, the Spirit of wisdom and understanding, the Spirit of counsel and might, the Spirit of knowledge and of the fear of the Lord (Isaiah 11:2 NKJV).

Father God, Your Word says, "the fear of the Lord is the beginning of wisdom; a good understanding have all those who do His commandments..." (Psalm 111:10 NKJV). Help me to know and keep Your commandments with praise and thanksgiving. Give me power when my heart is weak and strength when I have no might (Isaiah 40:29). I ask You to fill my mind with wisdom and my heart with understanding of You and Your ways (Job 38:36). Even in the night seasons, fill my dreams with instruction (Psalm 16:7). I want to know the hope of Your calling on my life, Lord (Ephesians 1:18).

I pray the Spirit of the Lord would inhabit my heart, mind, and voice. I desire the same wisdom, understanding, and "largeness of heart" that You blessed Solomon with (1 Kings 4:29 NKJV). I want to stand before You, God, for the sake of the people in my life. Let me bring their difficulties to You so they can be healed and made whole by Your wise counsel (Exodus 18:19). I will joyfully sit in the congregation and take counsel in the house of the Lord (Psalm 55:14). I will not only give wise counsel, but seek to increase learning. I will listen to those who fear You and are filled with Your Spirit (Proverbs 1:5).

King Jesus, give to Your servant an understanding heart to judge Your people rightly and with love. Help me discern between good and evil (1 Kings 3:9). I will keep Your law to love only You and Your people (Psalm 119:34) because "happy is the man who finds wisdom, and the man who gains understanding" (Proverbs 3:13 NKJV). Holy Spirit, pour out on me so I can lead my family with humility; serving them like Jesus. Show me how to put them first, ransoming them with my prayers, words, and selfless acts of redemption. I will bless and not curse them. I will speak life for Your glory and their destiny. I pray this in the name of Jesus Christ, amen.

SCRIPTURES

Isaiah 61:1 (NKJV) – *The Spirit of the Lord God is upon Me, because the Lord has anointed Me to preach good tidings to the poor; He has sent Me to heal the broken-hearted, to proclaim liberty to the captives, and the opening of the prison to those who are bound.*

Zechariah 4:6 (NKJV) – *So he answered and said to me: "This is the word of the Lord to Zerubbabel: 'Not by might nor by power, but by My Spirit,' says the Lord of hosts."*

James 3:13 (NKJV) – *Who is wise and understanding among you? Let him show by good conduct that his works are done in the meekness of wisdom.*

Proverbs 20:5 (NKJV) – *Counsel in the heart of man is like deep water, but a man of understanding will draw it out.*

Job 12:12-13 (NKJV) – *Wisdom is with aged men, and with length of days, understanding. With Him are wisdom and strength, He has counsel and understanding.*

Psalm 119:130 (NKJV) – *The entrance of Your words gives light; it gives understanding to the simple.*

Proverbs 17:27 (NKJV) – *He who has knowledge spares his words, and a man of understanding is of a calm spirit.*

Exodus 31:3 (NKJV) – *And I have filled him with the Spirit of God, in wisdom, in understanding, in knowledge, and in all manner of workmanship.*

Job 28:28 (NKJV) – *And to man He said, "Behold, the fear of the Lord, that is wisdom, and to depart from evil is understanding."*

I DECLARE IN THE MIGHTY NAME OF KING JESUS:

✝ I am strong in the Lord and in the power of His might (Ephesians 6:10). The Spirit of the Lord in me is liberty (2 Corinthians 3:17).

✝ The fear of the Lord gives me wisdom. Knowledge of the Holy One is understanding (Proverbs 9:10).

ᛏ The Issachar anointing belongs to me! I understand the times and seasons, and give wise counsel to both rich and poor (1 Chronicles 12:32).

ᛏ The Lord gives me wisdom and might. He makes mysteries known to me (Daniel 2:23).

ᛏ I do not have a spirit of fear, but of power, love, and a sound mind (2 Timothy 1:7).

ᛏ The Spirit of Counsel is mine, and sound wisdom. I am understanding; I have strength (Proverbs 8:14).

ᛏ I have heard the counsel of God. I do not limit wisdom to myself, but listen to those who also fear the Lord (Job 15:8).

ᛏ My mouth speaks wisdom. The meditation of my heart gives understanding to all who seek the Lord (Psalm 49:3).

ᛏ Your precepts give me understanding; therefore I hate every false way (Psalm 119:104).

ᛏ The peace of God, which surpasses all understanding, guards my heart and mind through Christ Jesus (Philippians 4:7).

Battle Cry for a Mother's Wisdom

For wisdom is better than rubies, and all the things one may desire cannot be compared with her (Proverbs 8:11 NKJV).

Lord God, Your Word says wisdom is a woman crying out by the open doors of Your saving grace. Today, let my voice echo hers calling people to "understand prudence...be of an understanding heart" (Proverbs 8:5 NKJV). Lord, fill me with wisdom to always speak what is excellent, right, and true for Your glory and to keep out of the pit. Wickedness is an abomination to my lips (Proverbs 8:3-7); I will speak blessings not curses, so my descendants will find life (Deuteronomy 30:19).

Lord, let this generation receive Your Word and treasure the commands of the wisdom you have put inside me. Incline my own ears to wisdom and apply my heart to understand Your heart and Your hand. I cry out for discernment. Lift my eyes to see from a higher perspective. I seek wisdom as silver and thank You for her hidden treasures placed in my life. Give me knowledge of You, Holy Spirit, so I can help the lost understand the fear of the Lord in this day (Proverbs 2:1-5).

Father God, fill my mind with understanding of You so I can give wise and godly counsel to those seeking You. Help them to receive the instruction of justice, judgment, and equity You have placed in me for their knowledge and discretion (Proverbs 1:1-5). I thank You for the elevated window of insight You have given me (Proverbs 1:2). Let it be a blessing to others and to You, King Jesus. Amen.

SCRIPTURES

Proverbs 1:7 (NKJV) – *The fear of the Lord is the beginning of knowledge, but fools despise wisdom and instruction.*

Proverbs 16:16 (NKJV) – *How much better to get wisdom than gold! And to get understanding is to be chosen rather than silver.*

Proverbs 3:16-18 (NKJV) – *Length of days is in her* **[wisdom's]** *right hand, in her left hand riches and honor. Her ways are ways of pleasantness, and all her paths are peace. She is a tree of life to those who take hold of her, and happy are all who retain her.*

Proverbs 4:7-9 (NKJV) – *Wisdom is the principal thing; therefore get wisdom. And in all your getting, get understanding. Exalt her, and she will promote you; she will bring you honor, when you embrace her. She will place on your head an ornament of grace; a crown of glory she will deliver to you.*

Proverbs 8:34 (NKJV) – *Blessed is the man who listens to me, watching daily at my gates, waiting at the posts of my doors.*

Proverbs 8:35-36 (NKJV) – *For whoever finds me* **[wis-dom]** *finds life, and obtains favor from the Lord; but he who sins against me wrongs his own soul; all those who hate me love death.*

Proverbs 11:2 (NKJV) – *When pride comes, then comes shame; but with the humble is wisdom.*

Proverbs 24:3-4 (NKJV) – *Through wisdom a house is built, and by understanding it is established; by knowledge the rooms are filled with all precious and pleasant riches.*

Proverbs 24:5-6 (NKJV) – *A wise man is strong, yes, a man of knowledge increases strength; for by wise counsel you will wage your own war, and in a multitude of counselors there is safety.*

Proverbs 29:11 (NKJV) – *A fool vents all his feelings, but a wise man holds them back.*

James 1:5 (NKJV) – *If any of you lacks wisdom, let him ask of God, who gives to all liberally and without reproach, and it will be given to him.*

James 3:17 (NKJV) – *But the wisdom that is from above is first pure, then peaceable, gentle, willing to yield, full of mercy and good fruits, without partiality and without hypocrisy.*

I DECLARE IN THE MIGHTY NAME OF KING JESUS:

† I am filled with wisdom because the Lord gives liberally to all who ask (James 1:5).

† My face shines with the wisdom of Christ in me (Ecclesiastes 8:1).

† I have ears to hear the Word of the Lord. I do as He commands and my house will not be shaken (Matthew 7:24).

† My adversaries cannot contradict or resist God's wisdom through me (Luke 21:15).

† I understand great mysteries and have prophetic revelation through Jesus Christ (Jeremiah 33:3; Daniel 2:22).

† I know the hope of my calling according to the working of His mighty power in me (Ephesians 1:16-19).

† I walk circumspectly, not as a fool. I redeem the time because the days are evil (Ephesians 5:15-17).

† I have a heart of wisdom. I number my days (Psalm 90:12) and refuse to take the name of Christ in vain (Exodus 20:7).

† The Spirit of the Lord rests upon me. The Spirit of wisdom and understanding, the Spirit of counsel and might, the Spirit of knowledge and of the fear of the Lord (Isaiah 11:2; Psalm 111:10).

CONCLUSION

While this devotional was meant to be a resource you could either read through as a monthly practice or turn to in a time of crisis, these prayers, Scriptures, and declarations all boil down to this—there are some things you have to decide not to give up. Come hell or high water, you will not give up. So, you stand. That's what you do.

You hold on to the righteousness of Jesus Christ when your child gets sick, when your job gets taken away, your marriage is on the rocks, or your money disappears. That's what it means to stand.

Listen, you don't have to stand for forever. You'll get to advance again—I promise you will. And this is how I know, because it happened to Moses and Joshua in Exodus chapter 17.

An evil king, Amalek, wanted to wipe out the children of Israel before they reached the Promised Land. Isn't that just like the enemy to try and kill the promise before it can manifest?

The Lord told Joshua to take his men and fight this highly skilled, better-armed fighting force. Then, God Almighty told Moses to hold his hands up high; and as long as he kept them up, Joshua would be victorious.

Now, think about what that looked like. It must have looked like Moses was holding up a banner! While his arms were raised, Israel was winning. If he got tired and they fell, the Amalekites would take ground. Aaron and Hur had to hold Moses's arms up, and the Lord gave them the victory.

Just like that, Jehovah Nissi will show up on your battlefield. The momentum will change. His banner will be seen and you'll say, "Dude, the King has shown up on my battlefield! He sees me and loves me because He fights for me."

When you use these prayers and declarations—when your raise your voice and your hands to Heaven for help—the momentum changes and Jesus brings you the victory. That's the whole understanding of Jehovah Nissi as "The Lord is our Banner."

> Then the Lord said to Moses, "Write this for a memorial in the book and recount it in the hearing of Joshua, that I will utterly blot out the remembrance of Amalek from under heaven." And Moses built an altar and called its name, The-Lord-Is-My-Banner **(Exodus 17:14-15 NKJV).**

What Amalekites need to be wiped off the face of your earth? What battle do you need the Lord to win on your behalf? My friend, you will get tired. The battle will take time, but put your hands in the air and call on Jehovah Nissi—The Lord Your Banner—to shift the momentum for your victory.

I call you the head, not the tail; above and not beneath, and highly favored of the Lord,

Troy

ABOUT
THE AUTHOR

Troy Brewer is the founding and senior pastor of OpenDoor Church in Burleson, Texas. He is known for his relevant and authentic teachings, amazing insights, and studies on the wonders of God including astronomy, numbers, typology, and times and seasons. He has a radical love for Jesus and a passion for serving people beyond the norm.

As a sixth-generation Texan and descendant of Henry Brewer, who fought at the battle of San Jacinto, Troy also has a passion for all things Texas. Troy has been married to his beautiful wife, Leanna, since 1989, has four grown children and six grandchildren.

Troy has a passion for "reaching Christians for Jesus" and is seen by a worldwide internet audience every Sunday and Wednesday from OpenDoor Church. His unique style and revelatory perspective brings clear and simple understanding to complex Kingdom issues and principles. He likes to say he has the "gift of realness," and that ability helps him reach both the lost and the saved with the transformational teachings of Jesus Christ.

Troy is a one-of-a-kind Christ follower—a true extension of the arms of Jesus. He is a servant whose greatest desire is to bring the authenticity of Jesus and the reality of the Kingdom of Heaven into the lives of people around the world.

An offshoot of OpenDoor Church in Burleson, Texas, Troy Brewer Ministries encompasses Troy's media and musical efforts to reach the lost and free the enslaved worldwide. To book Troy for a conference or speaking engagement, email info@opendoorexperience .com.

CONTACT INFORMATION

TroyBrewer.com

ODX.TV

OpenDoorExperience.com

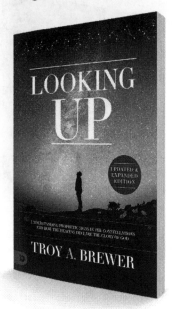

From

Troy A. Brewer

Redeem Your Timeline!

Haunted by your past? Anxious about the future? The omnipotent God of the Bible is not confined by the limits of time. He is not ashamed of your past or uncertain about your future. Every moment of your life is always held in the palm of His hand.

Troy Brewer – pastor of OpenDoor church, founder of Troy Brewer Ministries, and dynamic prophetic voice – shares a revolutionary teaching on your relationship to time.

As a believer, you can invite Jesus into your personal timeline to supernaturally redeem your past and miraculously prepare your future. Because past sins have been erased, the pain of trauma, abuse, and heartbreak can be redeemed. Future fears can be put to rest, as stress, anxieties, and uncertainties are surrendered to Him.

Discover the supernatural freedom that comes when Jesus enters your timeline!

Purchase your copy wherever books are sold

From

Troy A. Brewer

Powerful prayers and declarations that supernaturally redeem your past and miraculously prepare your future

In his bestselling book *Redeeming Your Timeline*, pastor and author, Troy Brewer showed you the radical transformation that is possible when you invite God into your personal history and timeline.

Now, in *40 Breakthrough Declarations*, Troy equips you with practical tools to reverse the plans of the enemy, release Heaven's healing power, and exchange the pain of your past for a glorious future filled with hope and purpose!

This powerful book features compelling devotionals and specific declarations to...

- Identify and break strongholds that hinder personal progress.
- Speak words that dismantle the enemy's lies.
- Experience divine reversals of hurt, shame, and pain as you apply Jesus' redemption to your past, present, and future.
- Prophesy hope and healing to places of trauma.

The Lord wants to bring redemption into every situation in your life, and He wants to partner with you to do it. Learn to speak the words that release His power over your timeline!

Purchase your copy wherever books are sold

Made in United States
Orlando, FL
20 January 2024

42645129R00089